A LIGHT FOR YOUR PATH

ANTON SAMMUT

A Light
for Your Path

Anecdotes, Thoughts, Prayers
and Quotations

ST PAULS

ST PAULS Publishing
187 Battersea Bridge Road, London SW11 3AS, UK

Copyright © ST PAULS 2000

ISBN 085439 614 4

Set by TuKan, Fareham, Hampshire, UK
Printed by Interprint Ltd, Marsa, Malta

ST PAULS is an activity of the priests and brothers
of the Society of St Paul who proclaim the Gospel
through the media of social communication

CONTENTS

CONTENTS

FOREWORD

I have been planning to write this book since the publication of my other book *Prayers and Thoughts for Students* in 1994. It was in my mind to procure another adequate book, but different in style and material, for the young adult students, boys and girls, for their school/college assemblies. No doubt, this book is not written exclusively for the students. Surely not! It can be used by anyone, young or old, at any time, anywhere, from being in the privacy of one's own room to being in the comfort of a rocking-chair on a veranda. Moreover, it is written in such a way that anybody adhering to any religious belief or denomination whatsoever may benefit from it.

The **anecdotes** are as concise as I could possibly make them. They are taken from various newspapers, magazines, books and even from hearsay. They just serve as a base to build up on them a relevant subject, which I tried to elucidate briefly in a **thought**, a **prayer**, and a suitably selected **quotation**.

With the exception of the names of the authors responsible for the **quotations**, no names of persons, places, countries or religions are used. In one anecdote only I used the name, and that is of the Lord Jesus Christ.

I have used the pronoun 'we' throughout, for the sake of the students gathered together during the assembly time. And every subject is set on two pages facing each other so that one need not turn the page.

May we realise that our life will be just as good (or bad) as we make it! We would do well if at times we stop and remind ourselves that we are in the presence of God; that no matter who we are or what we are, God is loving us, and is surrounding us with his care and guidance.

A Light for Your Path, is intended to help the practice of reflection and prayer, even on simple matters, thereby we will experience the growing reassurance that irrespective of our imperfections, difficulties and frailties, whatsoever they may happen to be, we are not alone.

I take this opportunity to show my sincere thanks and gratitude to Mr Carmelo Debono B.A., not only for his valuable suggestions and corrections he has done to my work, but also for the encouragement he has always given me.

Fr Anton Sammut

17TH CENTURY NUN'S PRAYER

Although this prayer is meant mainly for the elderly, young people, who will one day be themselves elderly, may find thoughts in it that are useful to them today.

Lord, Thou knowest better than I know myself, that I am growing older and older. Keep me from the fatal habit of thinking I must say something on every subject and on every occasion. Release me from craving to straighten out everybody's affairs. Make me thoughtful but not moody; helpful but not bossy. With my vast store of wisdom, it seems a pity not to use it at all, but Thou knowest, Lord, that I want a few friends at the end.

Keep my mind free from the recital of endless details; give me wings to get to the point. Seal my lips on my aches and pains. They are increasing, and love of rehearsing them is becoming sweeter as the years go by. I dare not ask for grace enough to enjoy the tales of others' pains, but help me to endure them with patience. I dare not ask for improved memory, but for a growing humility and a lessening cocksureness when my memory seems to clash with the memories of others. Teach me the glorious lesson that occasionally I may be mistaken.

Keep me reasonably sweet; I do not want to be a saint – some of them are so hard to live with – but a sour old person is one of the crowning works of the devil. Give me the ability to see good things in unexpected places, and talents in unexpected people. And give me, Lord, the grace to tell them so. Amen.

1

UNKIND WORD

A television newsreader was reading the news during a live teatime show when a fly flew into his mouth. His instinct was to spit it out but he felt that in doing so he would have disgusted most of the people watching him.

He did not want to make a scene especially knowing that the viewers were having their breakfast and could have been made ill.

Hence he choked on his words but just could not spit the fly out. He had to be professional, and therefore there was only one choice, swallowing the fly. That is what he did.

THOUGHT

There are times when we must defy ourselves and be brave enough to swallow, not flies of course, but words.

Occasions do come when we are tempted to use an unkind word, perhaps during a hot argument, when we get angry, in retaliation for an offence received, or even as a joke. Blessed are we if instead of letting it slip we bite our tongue and restrain ourselves from saying it.

Let us remember that unkindness hurts more than any other offence. Hence before we speak let us measure and weigh our words.

While the word is in our mouth, it is our own, it does no damage, but once it is spoken it may be very harmful. Just as one tiny spark can set on fire a great forest, similarly one word can do enormous damage.

PRAYER

O Lord God, may we have the insight to understand the responsibility of every word that we let go out of our mouth.

May we never be guilty of saying words that hurt, offend, harm, ridicule, deride, or in some way or other cause pain.

On the other hand, by the words we say may we be instruments that create an atmosphere of harmony, hope and healing all around us, especially among those who need it.

For the unkind words that we have unfortunately uttered in the past we regret, and now we are very determined not to say any such words in the future.

QUOTATION

Beat me but do not say an unkind word to me.

(Maltese Proverb)

2

FULFILLING OUR DUTIES WELL

ANECDOTE: GIRL FALLS THROUGH A BUS FLOOR HOLE

A three-year-old girl died when she fell through a hole in the floor of a bus which was running at a high speed.

In the accident that happened at midday, the child was crushed under the wheels of the same bus, and died instantly.

Photographs showed that the bus the child was travelling in, had a hole measuring 20 by 45 cm in the fourth row of seats.

The hole appeared partly covered with a rubber floor mat.

THOUGHT

It is very sad and very bad indeed that the person responsible for the comfort and safety of the passengers in the bus did not notice the dangerous hole.

Of course it would have been very shameful and also severely condemnable if the one in charge knew about the hole and still failed to remove the danger; the negligence causing the death of a child.

The tragedy of that little girl could have easily been

averted if the responsible person had fulfilled his duties conscientiously.

PRAYER

O Lord God, we earnestly pray for strength and courage to live well by fulfilling our duties to the best of our ability, whether we live for a short or a long time.

We fervently ask you to direct and guide us so that we will not live solely to ourselves. Let us be always conscious that besides having duties to perform towards ourselves, we have duties towards you also, and towards others as well.

Let us strive hard that we may never for a moment forget your presence so that we may always do our work as you would like it to be done; and that we may ever seek to find your will for us.

QUOTATION

A man must not be judged by the nature of his duties but by the manner in which he does them.

(Vivekananda)

3

CRUELTY TO ANIMALS

ANECDOTE: A PUPPY GIVEN AS A PRESENT

A four-year-old boy received a puppy as a present for his birthday. For about three weeks he was thrilled with his new friend. But then he got tired of it and neglected it.

The mother seeing that her child was no longer interested in the puppy and failing to look after it anymore, began to take care of it herself.

After some time she realized that by looking after it, she had increased her work at the cost of foregoing other much more important housework.

She began to grumble about it, and had even asked her husband to take the puppy by car to a very far distant place and leave it there to its fate.

That was exactly what at the end her husband did to please her. Most probably the puppy died by being run over or by starving.

THOUGHT

Cruelty to animals is not only beating them or torturing them. Giving them to little children as presents after passing an examination, for a birthday or for any other special occasion, is also cruelty to animals, because very often such children treat them as toys made of steel or plastic. Besides, as it often happens, the child, after a week or two, or a month or two gets fed up with it, and then discards it.

It is as bad when the animal is chased out of the house and left to fend for itself. It often becomes thirsty and hungry and it may even starve to death.

The animal cannot appeal for itself, it cannot complain, and that makes the cruelty all the worse.

PRAYER

O Lord God, we praise and thank you for creating such a vast variety of animals. We desire to share your love for all of them.

We want to tell you that we not only disassociate ourselves from those who hurt animals but we condemn them also. We feel very sorry for those animals that are suffering, over-worked, underfed, cruelly treated, hunted, lost, deserted, frightened or hungry.

We promise to be true friends to all animals.

QUOTATION

Animals are such agreeable friends – they ask no questions, they pass no criticisms.

(George Eliot)

4

ONE STEP AT A TIME

A well-known bacteriologist had a lady assistant working with him. One day, about three hundred samples of milk had arrived in one consignment into his laboratory for testing, which of course had to be done by the assistant.

The bacteriologist felt sorry for her having such an amount of work to do; so he told her: "Isn't all that testing far too much for you to do?"

"O no, Sir," she answered, "I'll just do them one at a time. There isn't a better way, as far as I know!"

The bacteriologist appreciating her answer, said: "You are very wise," and then to encourage her he continued: "After all, it is bite by bite that we finish eating a whole cake."

THOUGHT

When we have a great deal of work to perform, we should not just sit and stare at things and idle the time. In that case the work will not be done.

We should neither opt to do it in haste; haste is waste.

Let us keep in mind that when we find ourselves in

such situations, we must take up the work immediately but calmly.

Most of us, now and again, become overwhelmed with the things with which life confronts us. We must concentrate on what is to be done first, and then in a steady and unremitting effort we must start the work at hand. Steady perseverance will in the end achieve the desired results.

PRAYER

O Lord God, help us to keep our cool when we find ourselves in situations where we'll be loaded with lots of work, or perhaps with work which is hard and tedious.

While performing the work, however difficult it may seem to be, make us diligent, so that when afterwards we complete the work, we will have no cause to be ashamed of.

Let us also remember that we can turn our work into a prayer, that is, by doing it conscientiously for your honour and glory, and not just because it has to be done.

QUOTATION

The man who removed the mountain did so by carrying away small stones, one at a time.

(Chinese Proverb)

5

PUNCTUALITY

ANECDOTE: BUY A NEW WATCH

A famous President of a great nation had a secretary who had the habit of arriving late at the office for work.

One day the President waited at the door of the office for the secretary to appear.

When finally the secretary arrived, the President asked him: "May you please tell me why you are late?"

"Sir," he answered, "because my watch is not keeping good time."

"In that case," the President advised him, "you may either buy a new watch or else I'll get a new secretary."

THOUGHT

To be punctual means to be observant and exact in matters of keeping time and appointments.

Punctuality adhered to wins for us the respect of others. Punctuality not kept incurs the wrath of others upon us.

Once we accept a fixed appointment or a commitment, keeping our word is not optional but compulsory.

It is bad to waste one's own time, it is worse to waste that of other people. Indeed punctuality is a virtue.

PRAYER

O Lord God, by making punctuality our way of life we intend showing you how we appreciate the value of time which you so graciously give us continuously.

Help us to keep a disciplined punctuality in our schedule throughout the day right up to its end, deeming time very precious for ourselves and for others.

Let us remember that failing to be punctual is most unfair because thereby we waste the time of the other person, if not ours as well.

QUOTATION

Unfaithfulness in keeping an appointment is an act of clear dishonesty. You may as well steal a person's money as his time.

(Horace Mann)

6

DEATH

A very successful pop artist died in a motor vehicle accident while vacationing.

He suffered severe head injuries when the sports car he was driving pulled out onto a highway and was hit by a bus.

He was going to celebrate his 41st birthday in a week's time.

The artist oriented to play a synthesizer had already been acclaimed a classical prodigy before turning to the pop field.

He had a few hits on an international level, and he had well over a dozen CDs and videos on the market in his homeland. He was growing fast in popularity.

THOUGHT

Death is the event that terminates life. For us human beings, death is the ending of our temporary life in this world, and at the same time it is the beginning of our everlasting life in the world to come. It is actually a passage.

Death is the inescapable and inevitable destiny of all creatures. Yes, the fact of it is absolutely certain, but the time of it is very uncertain.

Death brings us face to face with God. Then we have to give Him an account of our life.

Let us therefore be wise enough to strive in living a good life in the sight of God.

PRAYER

O Lord God, help us never to forget how fast time flies. Help us to remember that we never know when, where and how our life will end. May we make the best out of every moment of the time we have at our disposal.

When, where and how we will die, is known to you alone. Help us to live this present moment well. If we are able to persevere in doing so throughout our life, we will have our mind at rest that whenever, wherever and however the end will come, it will be surely in our favour.

QUOTATION

Death never takes the wise man/woman by surprise; he/she is always ready to go.

(Jean de La Fontaine)

7

ADMITTING OUR FAULTS

ANECDOTE: SHE DID NOT UNDERSTAND

A husband, a stockbroker by profession, and his wife were one evening together in the sitting room reading the newspaper.

"What makes the stock market go up and down?" the wife asked.

He was quick to reply: "Socio-economic situation, inflationary pressures and fiscal instability. To these one may also add international imbalance and political tensions."

The wife did not understand. After pondering for a moment, she said: "If you really don't know, dear, why don't you say so?"

THOUGHT

The wife would have been more honest and praiseworthy if she had to admit that she had not understood what her husband had said, rather than accusing him that he was not capable of giving her the right answer.

Our corrupt nature is ever ready to blame others for our shortcomings and failures. It is so easy!

*No doubt, it takes courage to say that we are wrong,
that we are sorry!*

*There can be no peace of mind, neither forgiveness
nor amendment unless we admit our own fault and show
our sorrow for it.*

PRAYER

O Lord God, pardon us for the number of times we have
excused ourselves and blamed others for our wrongdoing.

If at any time we become well aware that we have
done something wrong, spare us from the wickedness of
putting the blame on somebody else. Give us the grace to
have the courage to admit our error.

Make us realise that though we may fool others we
can never fool you. Spare us from this foolishness of
trying to hide things from you.

You know us through and through, infinitely better
than we actually know ourselves.

QUOTATION

**Usually we have no difficulty in finding someone or
something to whom or to which the blame may be
attached.**

(William Barclay)

8

FRIENDSHIP

ANECDOTE: "I KNEW YOU'D COME"

During World War I, two young soldiers became close friends. When, after an unsuccessful night sortie, one of them was missing, the second youth asked for permission to go and search for his friend.

The commanding officer granted permission, but added: "It's not worth it. Your friend is probably dead by this time, and you will throw your life away."

The youth crawled out at the peril of his life to help his friend.

When, some time later, the rescuer returned, dragging the body of his dead comrade, and he himself mortally wounded, he looked up at his commanding officer and said with joy: "Sir, it was worth it. When I reached him, he looked at me and told me: "I knew you'd come.""

THOUGHT

Sometimes true friendship asks for the presence of a friend watching in silence near by.

There are other times when just to be close by with folded arms and to do nothing would not be an act of friendship at all; rather it asks for action, even to risk one's own life for the other.

A truly good friend knows which time is which, who knows when to give a helping hand and when just to stay close by.

Friends seem to have intuitive knowledge of each other's needs.

PRAYER

O Lord God, we want to thank you for all those whose friendship gives us daily support and whose love increases our happiness. We acknowledge that such a friendship is something very precious indeed.

We thank you for all the friends, without whom life could never be the same. May we remain always faithful to each other, and keep striving to strengthen our friendship.

Forgive us if we have worried or hurt any of them. We ask you to bless them and keep them safe.

May we be true friends to our friends.

QUOTATION

A friend is the one who comes in when the whole world has gone out.

(E. DeWitt Jones)

9

SELFLESSNESS

ANECDOTE: GIVING AWAY THEIR TOY CAR

Two little boys of the same age lived next door to each other. One of them received from his daddy a toy car, a real beauty indeed. The two played with it as if it belonged to both of them together.

One day the owner of the car broke the news to his friend that he had decided on his own accord to give the car to the children at the orphanage.

The other child said: "Why? Is it damaged or something wrong?"

"No! If it was so, I wouldn't give it. It is because their guardians cannot afford to buy them such toys."

Both the children took turns joyfully driving it on their way to the orphanage.

After giving it to the orphans they returned home very happy as if they had made a big bargain out of it.

THOUGHT

No doubt, it was a big sacrifice for the two boys to give up something, which was very dear to their heart, still, both of them did it willingly and gladly.

They had an aim in view. They wanted to make happy other children who were less fortunate than they were.

They had put into practice the real meaning of sacrificing something very dear to them to grow into a deeper experience of love.

After completing that sacrifice did they experience joy and contentment, which such acts bring along with them? Undoubtedly they did.

They had taught themselves the big lesson of "receiving in giving".

PRAYER

O Lord God, sometimes we are afraid of depriving ourselves of something dear to us for the sake of somebody else, because we think that it hurts us. We look at such sacrifice as a loss, instead of seeing it as a gain.

May we understand that selflessness frees us from selfishness. It strips us somehow from being self-centred.

Keep us from becoming complacent about the needs of others, rather help us in striving to achieve a personal concern for the needs of those around us.

QUOTATION

The man who lives for self alone, lives for the meanest mortal known.

(Joaquin Miller)

10

GOD IS OUR FATHER

ANECDOTE: TWO LITTLE BOYS MISTOOK BABY FOR A DOLL

A young mother was strolling in her house garden with her one-month-old baby for a breath of fresh air. After a little while she heard the telephone ringing. Thinking that she would only be away for a few minutes while her child was safely sleeping in the pram, she went to answer it.

On returning she was shocked to find her baby screaming in the hands of two small boys, her neighbours' children.

She thought that they must have played roughly with it because it had a few bruises on her face and hands. Questioning those two little boys why they had hurt her baby, they simply answered: "When we saw it alone having no mother, we thought it was a doll. And as we took it in our hands to play with it, it slipped and fell to the ground."

THOUGHT

It is almost unbelievable that the two boys had mistaken the baby for a doll. And yet we do come across children

who bully others, by being rough, unkind and even cruel.
Why children? There are adults who unfortunately treat
children worse than playthings, much worse. Let us hope
that we are not, and will never be among them.

We are all children of the same Father in heaven who
has created us in his image and likeness. Hence we are
brothers and sisters to each other.

When we take God out of our minds or forget about
him, then we also fail to treat others in the way that He
would like us to deal with each other.

PRAYER

O Lord God, we want to keep always in our mind that
the world in which we live is your handiwork, and that
wherever we go, we can assuredly say: "God, our Father,
is here."

In the same way, we want to keep in mind that all the
people – children, adults, grown-ups and seniors, among
whom we live and move, are all your children, hence our
beloved brothers and sisters.

Help us to treat each and every one who crosses our
path, as your child, a 'child of God', that is, with kindness,
patience, understanding and love.

QUOTATION

"Lord, I have a problem – it's me."
"My dear child, I have the answer – it's Me!
(Words of Wisdom – Daniel P. Cronin)

11

HONESTY

ANECDOTE: THE TRAFFIC POLICEMAN

A traffic policeman stopped the driver of a car and asked him for details to book him for excessive speed.

The driver was quick to present the badge showing that he was a traffic police sergeant of another zone in the country.

The policeman was taken aback and was rather sad that it had to be he who had to do that unpleasant job. In fact he told the sergeant: "How very sorry I am, but all the same I've to continue to fulfil my duty."

"My dear man," the sergeant replied, "I can understand what you are feeling right now in this awkward situation and I tell you that I am admiring you for your loyalty towards your duty. If ever you come to work under my supervision, I shall remember that you are an honest man."

THOUGHT

Honesty is a quality within us that urges us to be true to ourselves and to others. It is that ability within us to stand up for our convictions, to honour our commitments and to be faithful to our duties.

Honesty establishes our good reputation as respectable persons, highly principled and trustworthy.

Through honesty we see the self as it really is, accepting one's potentialities and limitations and not hiding them from others.

PRAYER

O Lord God, make us aware that if we want to be upright persons, it is absolutely necessary to be honest.

We pray to be able to practise the value of honesty and make it our way of life in the home, school, place of work and society.

Help us to carry out our tasks and assignments with honesty, shouldering full responsibility for all the work undertaken.

Enlighten our minds to realise the value of honesty in day-to-day life situations, and to develop a positive attitude towards it.

QUOTATION

At the heart of brotherhood is the need for inner honesty, an honesty which demands righteousness even when we are not observed.

(J. E. Lante)

12

FAITH

Once a young boy expressed his desire to his friends to learn to swim. Immediately one of them who was two years older and could swim, volunteered to teach him. So off to the sea they went.

On arrival, the friend whispered: "Now you must commit yourself to the water." But every time the boy tried, he found it hard to do, he rather failed. At first he struggled, but then he began to sink.

"You must cease struggling, the sea will bear you up if only you allow it by simply lying still, resting on its strength," his companion suggested again.

After repeating many attempts, he at last succeeded.

He simply gave himself up entirely to the sea, lying on his back in the confidence that the sea would bear him up without his own aid. And it really did.

THOUGHT

Faith is a complete trust or confidence in someone or something. It is the persuasion of the mind that a certain statement is true. Its primary idea is trust. A thing is worthy of trust when it is true.

Faith admits of many degrees up to full assurance, in accordance with the evidence on which it rests.

We may have great faith in someone or in something and less faith in another one or in another thing.

PRAYER

O Lord God, increase our faith in you. Our faith in you can never be great enough. There is always space and need to increase it.

With great faith we cast our troubles and problems upon you, thereby we get that peace of mind, which only you can give.

Help us in having full confidence that in the light or in the dark you will never leave us alone, nor forsake us, and that you will never let us go.

We want to show our faith in you by leaving ourselves and our beloved ones wholeheartedly and entirely to your care.

QUOTATION

Waiting for the morning to dawn, that is the attitude of faith.

(Hugh Thomson Kerr)

13

TELLING LIES

ANECDOTE: "I HAVE A TIGER"

A little girl had the bad habit of saying lies. Once on her birthday she received a kitten as a present and she went out telling all her friends that she had been given a tiger cub.

When the mother came to know what her daughter was uttering, she called her by her side and warned her: "How many times have I told you not to say lies? Go to your room and tell God that you are sorry, and promise that you will not say any lies in the future."

The child obeyed and went to her room and prayed. As she came out, her mother asked her: "Did you tell God you are sorry?"

The little girl answered: "Yes, I did. But I heard God telling me that sometimes He finds it hard to tell my pussy from a cub of a tiger, too."

THOUGHT

A lie consists in speaking a falsehood with the intention of deceiving. It is the most direct offence against the truth.

Whereas the purpose of speech is to communicate known truth to others, the lie leads others into error because it says things contrary to the truth.

No doubt the habit of telling lies should not only be discouraged but must be also condemned.

PRAYER

O Lord God, we thank you for giving us the gift of speech by which we can communicate what we have in our minds to others.

Grant unto us minds, which always seek the truth, and grant that we may stand by and face the truth even when it hurts us.

Give us the courage never to say lies not even to save ourselves from being rebuked or punished.

Forgive us for the times we allowed our lips not to speak the truth.

QUOTATION

A liar will not be believed, even when telling the truth.

(Aesop)

14

PERSEVERANCE

SHE BECAME A FAMOUS SINGER

A young girl went for her first singing rehearsal, but the director did not get a very good impression of her. In fact he told her: "It would be better for you to learn something else like painting or sculpture rather than singing. I am sorry to tell you that you don't have a good voice."

She did not lose heart and continued to study singing, putting herself heart and soul into it.

Slowly but steadily she succeeded to become a very famous singer.

THOUGHT

Perseverance is that steadfast pursuit of an objective. It is an unwillingness to give up.

What is the secret of perseverance? Love, loving the object we want to obtain. It helps us enormously in our persisting effort to achieve our object.

As we move on in life, we get so many opportunities by which we can do so much good to ourselves and to others. There will be no profit unless we do our part as best as we can and of course persist in dealing with them.

How many joys we miss through our lack of perseverance!

PRAYER

O Lord God, help us to be unshakeable in our perseverance to achieve our objective, big or small. Encourage us never to give in, and never to give up, but to keep at it until we succeed.

We fully know that you give us so many opportunities by which we can do so much good to ourselves and to others.

Help us to achieve our aims by pursuing them persistently, relentlessly and with determination unto completion.

QUOTATION

Perseverance is the real fuel of accomplishment.

(Anon)

15

PRAYERS

ANECDOTE: "I AM NOT SCARED IN THE DAYTIME"

A grandfather asked his little grandson: "Do you say your night prayers regularly?"

"Oh, yes, just before hopping into my bed!" the little smart boy replied.

"And your morning prayers, too?" his grandfather asked again.

"Why should I?" the child retorted arrogantly. "I'm not scared in the daytime."

THOUGHT

Like that little child many of us turn to God in prayer only when we need him, when something goes wrong, otherwise we do not pray at all; just as we call the doctor only when we are sick.

We should go to God as we would go to our father or to our mother. We go to our parents not only when we are after something, but also to show them our love, to thank them for their kindness to us, to share with them our joys and our sorrows, our successes and our failures.

Similarly, we should not go to God in prayer just for

begging. Let us go to him often, to love him, to praise him, to thank him, to show our trust in him.

Yes, and surely we pray also for his help, care and guidance.

PRAYER

O Lord God, you have made all things and made them well. We thank you for the night during which we sleep and rest, and for the day during which we study, work, and have some fun as well.

We want to praise you for the light and the dark; for the sunset and for the sunrise; for the stars and the moon and the sun, and for the innumerable things you have placed around us to admire and to use.

We ask you to forgive us for the number of times we have failed to thank you and show you our appreciation for all you are doing for us.

We wish to show our gratitude to you for keeping us always in your loving care.

QUOTATION

All things have a home; the bird has a nest, the fox has a hole, the bee has a hive. A soul without prayer is a soul without a home.

(Abraham Joshua Heschel)

16

RUDE WORDS

ANECDOTE: BIRD BLACKS OUT 500 HOMES

A bird fished a choice eel out of a bay and then dropped it on a power line causing a freak power failure in 500 homes. Meanwhile it also brought about a great deal of inconvenience to so many people.

The Electric Power Company officials issued a short statement saying: "While investigating the mysterious blackout, the Company inspectors found a 60 cm long eel charred on a 6,600-volt power line. With every probability, a kite, one of the large birds common in coastal areas, fished the 'anago' eel from a nearby fishing port and dropped it on the power line. The anago is the same slithery eel normally grilled for a popular sushi."

THOUGHT

We human beings have no beaks; we have mouths. From our mouths words slip out, not fish.

At times, words of thanks, of appreciation, of praise, of encouragement, come out; kind and courteous words!

Unfortunately at other times, especially in moments of anger, when we are hurt by others or when we think that things are not going to our liking, we let slip from our mouths unkind words, rude words, words that may cause sadness or harm to others.

Next time we are about to say something let us weigh our words. Let us remember that in as much as we can do lots of good, so also we can do lots of harm. Yes, not only to others but also to ourselves.

PRAYER

O Lord God, in our dealing with others make us courteous and kindly. Help us never thoughtlessly or deliberately to speak in such a way as to hurt the feelings of others.

Forgive us, we ask you, if ever, as most probably we have, by our words wounded another's heart.

Be on our lips that we may always speak in such a way that we will bring nothing but joy and happiness to all those whose friendship is our delight.

QUOTATION

Be careful of the words you say, so keep them soft and sweet,
You never know from day to day which ones you'll have to eat.

(Marcus Allen)

17

REMEMBER TO PRAY

ANECDOTE: PUSHING HIS SHOES UNDER THE BED

An eleven-year-old boy, before going to sleep for the night, had the habit of pushing his shoes right under the bed somewhat out of manageable distance.

Evidently, on every morrow, he had to trouble himself going down on his knees in order to fetch them back.

This day-to-day habit annoyed his mother and one morning she could not help but murmur scoldingly: "Please have some sense! Keep your shoes where you can easily reach them. Thus you will save yourself of such an inconvenience every morning."

The child replied: "Because when I go down on my knees to get them, I remember that I've to say a short morning-prayer."

THOUGHT

That youngster made his own invention to remind himself to pray.

If only we make up our mind to think often of God, there are so many ways and instances that could remind us to pray!

When we look at a flower, which happens quite often, and we admire its shape, its colours, its scent, we could remind ourselves of the source of its beauty, and if we attribute it to God, that would be a prayer. So also when we hear a bird singing, if while admiring it we give praise to God, that would be a prayer. Seeing a sky lit up by thousands of twinkling stars would remind us of the source of its grandeur, and if we acknowledge that it is the handiwork of God, that would be a prayer.

Let us not allow a single day to pass without saying a prayer at least once.

Prayer

O Lord God, all-powerful and ever-living Father, we do well always and everywhere to think of you in prayer.

Teach us to pray, to want to pray, to delight to pray. Teach us to pray with faith, with hope, with love.

We are happy to be talking to you right now, we want to make it a point that we will talk to you again and again as the day goes by.

Quotation

He who has learned how to pray has learned the greatest secret of a holy and happy life.

(William Law)

18

PAIN AND SUFFERING

ANECDOTE: THE PAINTER WITH STIFFENED FINGERS

A famous painter, although advanced in age and sickly, continued to paint till the very end of his life.

But above all, he suffered from arthritis, which stiffened his fingers. As a result of which it was very painful for him to paint.

One day, when a friend saw him painting with much difficulty, pleaded with him to stop painting anymore.

The great artist replied: "The pain that I am suffering now passes away, but the beauty that I am creating on the canvas will last."

THOUGHT

There is a difference between pain and suffering. Pain is that sensation experienced when the body is injured or afflicted by certain diseases.

Suffering hits us when we not only undergo pain, but when we wonder how we are going to get through. Suffering becomes more acute when after trying our best without success to get rid of the pain, we do not endure it.

We should be wise to realise that when we are not able to remove the pain, then we have no other reasonable way than to accept what cannot be changed. Otherwise we will be loading on ourselves heavier burdens than the ones we already have.

PRAYER

O Lord God, guide us so that we do not make things for ourselves worse than they need to be.

We do understand that you do not want us to have pain and to suffer. Actually, to speak in human terms, while we have pain and are suffering, you suffer and cry with us.

If ever we have to pass through some difficult experiences, help us so that we will not rebel against the unavoidable pains and suffering. Do not let us despair, but let us learn to see what good we can get out of them.

We wish to commend to you all who are afflicted and distressed; comfort them and relieve them, and grant them your love and compassion.

QUOTATION

People are not responsible for all their suffering, of course, but they might be responsible for a good deal of it.

(Kenneth E Grabner)

19

BAD LANGUAGE

ANECDOTE: THE PARROT THAT COULD TALK

A rich man was once attracted by a beautiful parrot, which could even talk. On taking it home, after buying it, unfortunately he realised that it was accustomed to say bad words.

Its new owner was very upset about it because he did not want it to repeat those filthy words. So he thought of a scheme.

Whenever the parrot used good language the owner would give it new seeds, and whenever the parrot uttered bad words the man would give it a slight electric shock.

At last, after quite some time, the parrot learnt to curb its tongue.

THOUGHT

The language is the method of human communication, either by spoken or written words. It is a gift of God. It is actually a very great gift, since it marks us off from the animals.

Unfortunately, there are some of us who misuse it by using bad language.

There are varieties of bad language, such as swearing i.e. taking an oath on something sacred; blaspheming i.e. to utter profane words against God or anything sacred; cursing i.e. to invoke harm or evil on people.

Our language may also be obscene, foul, vulgar, profane, etc.

PRAYER

O Lord God, help us to think before we speak, so that we may never use bad language in any of its forms.

Give us that wisdom by which we know when to speak, and to speak in such a way that it will be pleasing to you; otherwise to keep silent.

Forgive us if ever we have uttered words that we should never have allowed them to soil our lips. We assure you that we wish we had never spoken such words at all, and we promise you to try our level best never to repeat them.

QUOTATION

May my spoken words and unspoken thoughts be pleasing even to you, O Lord my Rock and my Redeemer.

(Psalms 19:14)

20

RESISTING EVIL

ANECDOTE: THE ROBBER

After taking part in an armed robbery a young man returned home to evaluate the robbed portion allotted to him. He was greatly disturbed when all of a sudden he realized that his driving licence was missing from his pocket.

He rightly guessed that in his hurry to get away as fast as he could it had dropped from his pocket.

When the police came knocking at his door, he was not the least bit surprised. Actually he was expecting them to do so.

THOUGHT

Usually robbers are not so easily caught as this one. All the same, wrongdoers are often the victims of their own misdeeds. Somehow or other their evil doing catches up with them, not necessarily in a short time, or by being caught by the police.

Of course, we should not avoid doing evil so that we will not have to pay for our mischief. Rather we should shun evil for the simple reason that we must not perpetrate evil.

48

However, we should not be satisfied merely by not giving in to evil. We should use our whole energy in doing good wherever we are, at home, in the school, at work, in places of entertainment, whenever we get the opportunity.

PRAYER

O Lord God, from our own personal experience, even though we may be still young, we know how the wrongdoing comes out of us with ease, how strongly the evil things entice us towards them, and how much the forbidden things attract us.

We truly desire that we could tell you that we shall never allow ourselves to succumb to evil. But we are fully aware of our weakness and frailty.

Still we want to promise you with all our heart that we will make every effort within our power to keep ourselves away from whatever is evil and to do always what is right.

QUOTATION

Follow only what is good. Remember that those who do what is right prove that they are God's children; and those who continue in evil prove that they are far from God.

(3 John 11)

WORK

ANECDOTE: IF WE LAY LAZY

One Monday morning, before going to the factory, a young man mused to himself: "I wish I were a rich man! Then I wouldn't go for work."

It was still seven o'clock when he had already had a wash, brushed his teeth, shaved, prepared a few sandwiches, wrapped them up, tied them on his motor cycle and left for work.

He reached a little bit early. His companions arriving one by one, all seemed to have a gloomy face on that black Monday morning.

Meanwhile he recollected: "Without man's work, the world would be in a chaos! I wouldn't have had water, soap, bread, butter, clothes, shoes, and a motor cycle!" This thought made him enter into the factory cheerful and happy.

"What's the matter with you? Have you won the national lottery?" his fellow workmen teased him.

"I haven't won any money at all. I've just pondered how hard life would be if all of us didn't work and just lay lazy."

Thought

All of us have to do some kind of work or another to justify our existence. Every individual must contribute towards the betterment of society.

Work is performed not only by factory workers; students for instance also work. Study is their main work.

Besides, students work in keeping their classrooms and the school/college compound clean and tidy, they give a helping hand in the many activities of the school/college, and so on. The home also provides them with basic opportunities for work experience such as running on errands, cleaning, cooking, shopping, repairing and other chores.

Prayer

O Lord God, we thank you for enabling us to work and to find fulfilment in performing it.

May we appreciate more deeply what we are able to do. We feel proud when other people also benefit by our work.

We want to show our gratefulness for the many benefits we have received from the work of others.

Quotation

The truth is I am a very ordinary person, and if I have any success it is only due to hard work.

(Lord Louis Mountbatten)

TRUST IN GOD

ANECDOTE: A CHILD'S TRUST IN HER FATHER

A house was on fire. Some of the inmates were caught inside it and could not escape.

A little girl who happened to be inside at the time, bewildered in the smoke, appeared in a window, the fire roaring beneath.

A man in the crowd calling her by her name shouted in tones of agony: "I am your father: jump into my arms. Trust yourself in me."

The girl heard that voice, and she knew it. Hesitating for a moment, she seemed to fear. "I can't see you clearly," she said.

"But I can," again shouted the voice. That assured her. She jumped blindly, and was caught, slightly hurt, but saved.

THOUGHT

Trust is a firm belief in the reliability, truth, strength, etc. of a person or thing. That little girl had full trust in her father. In fact she threw herself blindly into his arms, and she was saved.

How often do we ask for God's help and then we tell him how He should go about giving it! That surely shows no trust in God. That is demanding. That is instructing the great God how he should respond to us. It is not asking for God's will to be done. It amounts to giving orders to God.

PRAYER

O Lord God, we want to abandon ourselves completely into your hands. We pray that your will be done, that your plans be accomplished, and that we want to place ourselves at your service.

We want to surrender ourselves into your hands, because we know that as our Father in heaven, you have our best interest at heart.

Make us ever to remember that you see us, and in you we live and move and have our being.

QUOTATION

Trust is the greatest joy in our relationship with God. Whoever trusts in God has already covered the hardest part of the journey. God, you are my God, I can count on you.

(Carlo Carretto)

23

TIME

ANECDOTE: "WHAT IS THE TIME?"

A man whose job was to punch the tickets of the people entering into the cinema hall, got fed up by the people asking him: "What is the time?"

So he thought of putting a stop to this nuisance.

He bought a big clock and hung it on the wall behind him where every one could see it.

But what happened? The people, after looking at the clock, began to ask him: "Is that clock correct?"

THOUGHT

Time is the indefinite continued progress of existence. Undoubtedly we cannot stop it, it keeps on passing; but we surely can make good use of it.

Every minute that passes will never come back again. If we waste it, it will be lost forever. It is a minute less in our lifetime. It is a minute closer to our end in this life.

Unfortunately we take time for granted and waste so much of it.

Let us remember that if we love our life, as we surely

do, then we should not squander time, for that is the stuff life is made of.

PRAYER

O Lord God, help us to realise that the time you give us is a daily miracle. We wake up in the morning, and lo! our suitcase is magically filled with twenty-four hours at our disposal. It is ours, the most precious of our possessions because it is as precious as life itself.

Help us to use it wisely, in such a way as you would like us to make use of it, without wasting a single second.

We promise to do our best to utilise the time at our disposal always with profit.

QUOTATION

Time is the deposit each one of us has in the bank of God and no one knows the balance.

(Ralph. W. Sockman)

24

HELPING OTHERS

ANECDOTE: A GIRL TEACHES HER CLASSMATE

A bright girl accepted wholeheartedly to teach a lesson in mathematics to a classmate who did not attend the teacher's lesson in class because of her absence from school due to illness.

Afterwards the girl said: "Teaching the lesson to my classmate was worthwhile on two scores. Firstly, I rendered a good service to her by helping her to learn the lesson. Secondly, thereby I have understood and grasped the lesson better myself."

THOUGHT

It is a fact that the best way to learn something is to teach it to someone else. Let us keep in mind that whatever the knowledge is, when we share it with someone else we grasp it better.

In imparting our knowledge to others, we enrich our own. However let us keep in mind that we enrich our life not only by imparting our knowledge to others, but even more so when we serve and show compassion and help others.

It is good to know that it is very rewarding to pass to others whatever good we can.

PRAYER

O Lord God, teach us to be as interested in giving, at least as much as we are in getting.

We pray to have the courage to give and keep giving, no matter what inconvenience or sacrifice we will have to undergo.

Let us realise that if it was not for your goodness and the goodness of others to help us, our own life would not have been as good as it is.

We admit that much of what we do is done more out of self-interest than out of genuine love.

May we succeed in cultivating the virtue of helping and serving others without having in mind the thought of gaining anything for ourselves.

QUOTATION

Help thy brother's boat across, and lo! thine own has reached the shore.

(Old Hindu Proverb)

25

CALAMITIES
BY NATURAL CAUSES

ANECDOTE: A WOMAN SWEPT BY MUD

Storms hammered the hometown of a twenty-eight-year-old woman, causing a torrent of mud and water to seep into her house.

She was sleeping then, but the thunderous noise made her wake up to rush towards the door, open it and let the mud pass through. It was at this time when she was hit by the full force of the torrent, which carried her out into the street causing her untimely death.

Her husband managed to save their four-year-old daughter, but he was unable to reach his wife. Her body was found about 200 metres from the house under a wrecked car that had also been carried off.

THOUGHT

The sea, the wind and the fire remind us of God's Power – overwhelming, irresistible. How foolish it would be of us to put ourselves up against God!

Not that we should think of storms, earthquakes, floods

and other calamities as specially caused by God to harm us. No, they are not. They are like the rest of the weather, inevitable results of natural causes. Spring, summer, autumn and winter follow each other in a natural way. Actually it would need a miracle to stop them working as they do.

PRAYER

O Lord God, we know that you have made the natural causes. Whatever we may say about the reason why you have made them the way they are, the mystery remains. In the meantime we can only guess.

The fact that you did create this kind of world tells us that somehow there is value in trials, suffering and sorrow.

Out of these, stem out courage, charity, kindness, self-sacrifice, which are so precious to you.

Help us to be always ready to rush to the help of those who fall victims to the cruelty of nature, and show kindness and generosity to them.

QUOTATION

The soul would have no rainbow had the eye no tears.

(John Vance Cheney)

26

PATIENCE WITH THINGS

ANECDOTE: SHE DID IT ALL OVER AGAIN

A woman, having done a big washing, hung it on a line to dry. It so happened that after some time the line broke and practically all her washing fell in the mud, but she did not utter a word.

Soon she did the washing all over again. Seeing that the line was not strong enough, she spread the washing on the ground. That night a dog walked over it with his muddy feet.

When she saw it, she kept calm. All she said was: "Isn't it funny, he didn't miss a piece!"

THOUGHT

Patience is the capacity of being able calmly to endure difficult situations without complaint.

It is the ability to cope up with the trials and reverses of life which cannot be changed.

It helps us to face the vicissitudes of life with courage and determination.

Contrary to what many people think, patience is strength not weakness, as someone has said that with patience we can do much more than with strength and fury.

PRAYER

O Lord God, knowing very well how easy it is to find ourselves in difficult situations, help us when we are in such predicaments to pass the breaking point and not to break.

We do not ask you to help us to do anything startling or heroic. We just beg you to help us to bear things without grumbling, without complaining, without whining, without self-pity.

In times of trials make us brave so that like good soldiers we will not succumb but triumph, and when they are over we will have every reason to rejoice.

QUOTATION

When I pause the longest, I make the most telling strokes with my brush.

(Leonardo Da Vinci)

27

TRIALS OF LIFE

ANECDOTE: DURING AN EXAMINATION

Just before Christmas a student was sitting for an examination. He did not know how to answer the question: "When did World War One break out?"

After pondering for some time he wrote:

(a) God knows when.
(b) I do not know.
(c) A happy Christmas.

A few days later, the student received the result with the following remarks:

(a) God gets hundred per cent marks.
(b) You receive a zero.
(c) A bright New Year.

THOUGHT

Students would consider themselves very lucky, if by chance they come to know the questions for the final examination. They would study the answers thoroughly to try getting full marks.

Our life is a trial and therefore it is a continuous examination. The questions, like that of the student, are also about past events, but they concern only our own past.

Moreover, we ask the questions ourselves, questions concerning us, such as: Why did we say that word? What made us react in that way?

PRAYER

O Lord God, help us to examine ourselves every now and again not to bewail the past. No! That would be useless, but to learn from it, so that our life may improve.

Give us your help so that we may remove every obstacle in our way lest we stumble, and slowly perhaps, but courageously, we uproot that which is evil in us; hence when we come face to face with small or even great trials we will not falter.

May our trials make of us wiser persons so that we may manage to lead a better and happier life.

QUOTATION

The gem cannot be polished without friction, nor man perfected without trials.

(Confucius)

28

WRONG CONCLUSIONS

ANECDOTE: BOEING 777 ENGINE CATCHES FIRE

One bright Sunday morning, shortly after take-off from the airport, an engine of an Air Boeing 777 caught fire.

The aircraft had been two minutes into its flight at 680 metres at 02.20 a.m. (1820 GMT) when it was shaken by three explosions from its right engine.

"At first I thought there was a hijacker causing some mischief on board the plane. Soon I realized that it was absolutely not so," the captain said.

The aircraft was carrying 109 passengers, and 15 crew. No one was injured.

THOUGHT

How often do we jump into the wrong conclusion, at times to our own detriment and to that of others!

Our conclusions may be wrong, as so often they are. "This is so," we say, "and this is so, and therefore this must also be so." Though in all appearances it seems to be so, yet no, it may not be so. Only God knows for sure what is right and what is wrong.

One of the grim facts of life is that most of us are so

prone to attach ill motives to others and to accuse them
of wrongdoing.

PRAYER

O Lord God, give us the grace to be always very careful in coming to a conclusion about someone else.

Make us to realise that every person is a walking paradox; every one of us is capable of being a saint and a sinner, sweet and harsh, understanding and condemning.

We know that only you can see the hidden possibilities in us. We see only outwardly, you see also inwardly. You see the side that no one of us can see.

QUOTATION

"Great spirit, help me never to pass a judgement on another until I have walked two weeks in his moccasins*."

(A prayer of Sioux Indians)

---

* Moccasins are shoes worn by North American Indians

29

APPRECIATION

ANECDOTE: BOY'S HEART SAVES GIRL'S LIFE

The heart of a boy killed in a road accident has given a
new lease of life to a girl.

"I assure everybody that she got a wonderful heart
both from nature's standpoint and from an emotional
standpoint," said the father, who donated the heart of his
son who was hit and killed by a car while crossing the
street with his bicycle six days before his ninth birthday.

The surgeon who performed the transplant said that
the recipient, a three-year-old child, had a heart three
times the normal size and would surely have had a limited
life without the transplant.

When the girl's mother was interviewed on a radio
station, along with the boy's father, she said with tears in
her eyes: "I am very thankful to him. He has helped my
daughter to live."

THOUGHT

*Appreciation is that readiness to show gratitude for a
favour or kindness received. It is a grateful recognition
and an inclination to return kindness.*

We cannot live solely on our own. Our life is full of situations that can get the best of us or challenge the best that is in us, hence we often need others' help and therefore we are so often on the receiving end.

To be appreciative fosters satisfaction not only in those to whom appreciation is shown but also in those who give it. Let us develop an appreciative heart in all circumstances. Let it become in us a way of life.

PRAYER

O Lord God, arouse in us a consciousness of being indebted to others for their kindness and sympathy towards us. At the same time awaken in us the urge to work in turn for the good of our fellow human beings on the principle of 'Having freely received, we will freely give".

Grant each one of us the gift of a grateful heart.

QUOTATION

Many times a day I realise how much my own outer and inner life is built upon the labours of my fellowmen, both living and dead, and how earnestly I must exert myself in order to give in return as much as I have received.

(Albert Einstein)

30

DILIGENCE

A passenger train collided with a horse-drawn cart killing eight people, six died on the spot and two at the hospital.

The police spokesman commenting on the incident said that it was due to the cart's driver failing to stop at a level crossing because he miscalculated the speed at which the train was running.

Horse-drawn carts are a major means of transport in rural regions of that country and sometimes they pose a serious hazard on the roads.

Thought

The cart driver should not have taken the risk of crossing at that particular moment at all.

Diligence consists in being careful and steady in carrying out our tasks and duties. Surely, if we want to perform well whatever work we decide to take into our hands, it is absolutely necessary for us to do it with great diligence.

By applying ourselves diligently to the work at hand

we will undoubtedly bring it to a satisfactory and a fruitful fulfilment.

Diligence is the mother of good luck.

PRAYER

O Lord God, we humbly ask you to help us to approach our work and our tasks diligently and cheerfully.

Equip us with the diligence, the perseverance, and the reliability, which will enable us to be good workers, and to perform our tasks to the best of our ability.

We thank you for the kindness, assistance, and co-operation we get from you and from others in carrying out our daily work up to its satisfactory completion.

QUOTATION

No amount of fine feeling can take away the place of faithful doing.

(William Barclay)

31

PATIENCE WITH OTHERS

ANECDOTE: ON BECOMING A PREFECT

A student was chosen to be the Prefect of the college. At his first meeting with his schoolmates he remarked: "Patience and understanding! I'll try my level best to be very understanding, and to be as much patient as possible with each and every one of you. Meanwhile I expect a reciprocal attitude towards me by all of you."

Years later, one of those college students became the Manager of the Firm where the one who was once his Prefect was employed. The first words uttered by the new Manager were: "Patience and Understanding!"

THOUGHT

Patience strengthens our self-control thereby helping us to withstand petty annoyances, provocations and indignations.

Through patience we accept people for what they are, and get resigned and tolerant of their weaknesses, defects and faults.

By cultivating patience, thereby making it to grow steadfast within us, we develop an attitude of bearing calmly the trials and the reverses of life that cannot be changed.

Indeed patience is the ability to endure the hurts caused to us by others, without retaliating.

PRAYER

O Lord God, help us to be always patient and understanding with others as well as with ourselves.

Never permit us, not even for a very short moment, to lose our temper, or to lose our head or to lose our heart. We know that left to ourselves, it is so easy to lose any of them.

May we have a heart that never hardens, a temper that never tires, and a touch that never hurts.

QUOTATION

The sign of true manhood is when you can keep your head while all about you are losing theirs and blaming it on you.

(Kipling)

32

CONCERN FOR OTHERS

ANECDOTE: TEARFUL FAREWELL

An heroic teacher and two girls were buried as hundreds of people gave a tearful farewell to the last of five killed in a schoolyard ambush that shocked the nation.

The people paid an emotional tribute to the 32-year-old lady killed when she jumped in front of her students aged between 11 and 13 to shield them from gunfire.

"Others are alive today because of her. The word hero has been used a lot lately, but if you want to see a real hero, if you want to hear the voice of an angel, if you want to look courage in the eye, then look no farther than this young teacher," the Headmistress told the mourners.

The teacher was married with a 2-year-old son.

THOUGHT

This teacher is an excellent example of one who shows a very deep concern for others. She even gave her life that her students might live.

By concern we mean involving oneself or taking solicitous interest in the welfare of others.

Concern for others often demands forgetting oneself even at the cost of making big sacrifices for others' sake.

PRAYER

O Lord God, grant that we may neither be too busy nor too tired, never too immersed in our own affairs and never too fond of our pleasure, to help those who need help.

Make us think of the needs of others, at least as much as we think of ours.

Help us to be a comfort to the sad; to be friendly to the lonely; to be an encouragement to the dispirited; to be a help to those who are in need of it; in short let us never lose any opportunity to offer consolation to the afflicted.

Bless all those who show concern for others; and forgive us for any concern we might have shown and did not.

QUOTATION

No man has learned to live until he can rise above the narrow confines of his individualistic concerns to the broader concerns of his fellowmen.

(Martin Luther King)

33

CONSEQUENCES OF OUR DEEDS

ANECDOTE: ASTEROID TO MISS THE WORLD

An asteroid, (that is one of the small planets that revolve round the sun mainly between orbits of Mars and Jupiter) which is headed towards Earth is not going to hit us after all, NASA said on Thursday 12th March 1998.

It would miss the planet by 960,000 km, NASA researchers said. The International Astronomical Union (IAU), which keeps track of such objects, said that an asteroid would pass very close to the Earth in the year 2028 and might conceivably hit it.

The IAU appealed for astronomers to have a look at the asteroid, dubbed 1997XF11, and see if they could get more information about its size and orbit.

THOUGHT

The NASA researchers are looking at what might happen when, after a few years, asteroids may come close to the world.

We too would do well to look at the future of our own

lives. We would be spared a number of inconveniences, and we would spare ourselves much worry and grief, if we cared to think how the things we are doing would look not at the present moment, but in another month or another year or perhaps even at the end of our life.

Let us keep in mind that a thing which may be very enjoyable while we are at it, may perhaps bring much regret and sorrow in the years to come.

PRAYER

O Lord God, make us understand that a thing attains its real significance and proportion only when we take the long view of it.

Make us wise enough to keep in mind that the consequences of our actions will continue to work and have repercussions long after their execution.

Help us to think not only of the future as it affects ourselves, but also as it affects others.

QUOTATION

Think always what may happen after, for what comes after cannot be brought before.

(Maltese Proverb)

34

OPTIMISM

ANECDOTE: FLOWER FACING THE LIGHT

A professor bought a plant and kept it on the window-sill of his study. After a few days a flower blossomed and the professor turned the pot in such a way that the flower would face towards the inside of his study so that he would admire its beauty even better while at work. But soon the flower took its previous position facing outside.

In spite of turning the pot again and again, the professor did not succeed in keeping the flower facing towards the inside of his study. Every time it turned again towards the bright light coming from outside the window.

THOUGHT

We can learn a great lesson from the behaviour of the flower, that is, we also should always try to look at the bright side of life. That is optimism.

Optimism is that inclination to take bright views in all matters. Hence an optimist makes 'the best of it even when he gets the worst of it'.

One who sees opportunity in every calamity, he/she is

an optimist; one who sees calamity in every opportunity, he/she is a pessimist.

Let us not be intimidated by difficulties, rather let us stand up manfully with resolute determination to surmount them.

PRAYER

O Lord God, help us to be among those who will light a candle rather than curse the dark.

Encourage us to make a good effort whenever we come to do something which may seem to be hard for us, but in fact well within our power.

Enable us to see the brighter sides of life. Let us also be fully aware that every cloud has a silver lining.

Make us ever deeply conscious that you are really on our side and always near as we tread along the strenuous paths of life.

QUOTATION

Keep your face to the sunshine and you cannot see the shadow.

(Helen Keller)

35

THE GIFT

ANECDOTE: THE SOLDIER WHO CAME HOME

The parents of a young man killed in the war presented a gift to one of the local philanthropic societies in their son's memory.

Seeing this kind gesture, the mother of another youth asked her husband to do a similar thing for their son.

"But our son came home," the father replied.

"That's just the point," the mother insisted. "Let us make a gift to show our appreciation for his coming home."

THOUGHT

The gift may be very good and beautiful, but the spirit that accompanies it, is undoubtedly more significant and important.

For the receiver, the value disappears out of a gift however valuable it is in itself, when happiness is not shown by the giver while giving it; likewise for the giver when no appreciation is shown by the receiver while receiving the gift.

There is as much nobility of heart in the

acknowledgement of a gift received as much as there is in the act of bestowing it on others.

We tend to look more at the heart than at the gift itself.

PRAYER

O Lord God, we want to offer to you our sincere thanks not only for the great gift of life you have given to us but also for what you have accomplished in us. Your power within us is actually another very big gift to us, for which we want to thank you also whole-heartedly.

Again, we want to give you thanks with great appreciation for the precious gift you have given us, in enabling us in doing whatever we have done so far in our life time for your greater glory, for our own good and for the good of others.

We wish that you would regard as our gift to you the acceptance of life and your power working within us.

QUOTATION

The manner of giving is worth more than the gift.

(Pierre Corneille)

36

RETURNING FOUND ARTICLES

ANECDOTE: HAVE YOU LOST YOUR DIARY?

According to a list published in the Government Gazette
of a very small Island there are the names of about fifty
people who handed in lost items to the police during the
months of July, August and September of 1997.

There were several items of cash as well as jewellery,
especially bracelets, cameras, watches, and wallets.

Other items raise curiosity, such as the pair of shoes,
vest and shampoo. And if one is living in fear of one's
own darkest secrets being found out, there may be hope:
a diary was also handed in to the police in September.

THOUGHT

*Probably all of us, some time or another, have lost
something or other. Whether the thing we lost was big or
small we surely had that strong desire to find it, especially
if it was of some importance or had a sentimental value
attached to it.*

*Surely, it is not a pleasure for us to lose anything, we
become sad depending on the value of the thing, but how
happy we are when we manage to find it! How grateful*

we feel towards the one who has found it and was kind
enough to return it to us!

We must keep in mind that what we ourselves feel,
with every probability others also feel, and hence when
we find something that does not belong to us we must try
our best to return it to its owner.

PRAYER

O Lord God, help us never to succumb to the temptation
to keep for ourselves anything, knowing that it belongs
to somebody else.

Convince us that a thing, which does not belong to us,
will never become ours by just keeping it; it will keep on
calling its rightful owner.

Let us also understand the pleasure we give to its
owner when we return it, and also the satisfaction it
brings into our own heart.

QUOTATION

To pretend to satisfy one's desires by possession is
like using straw to put out a fire.

(Chinese Proverb)

37

DETERMINATION

ANECDOTE: THE WOODCHUCK

Once there was a woodchuck. The woodchuck is a marmot, a species of animal that has strong short feet and long claws adapted for digging because it lives in burrows. Everyone knows that it doesn't climb trees. But one day a woodchuck was chased by a dog. It ran as fast as its legs could carry it until it came to a tree.

"If I can only get up this tree," it said to itself, "I'll be safe, otherwise I'm doomed."

It had to get up there to save its life, so it did.

THOUGHT

Determination is that ability which drives us to pursue our aim up to the very limit regardless of any opposition that we may encounter.

True determination is indomitable and relentless in its endeavour to achieve its aims and purposes; it yields to nothing until its goal is attained.

Determination helps us a great deal in overcoming our own physical and mental handicaps, thereby we achieve what often seems impossible.

PRAYER

O Lord God, instil into each and every one of us the conviction and determination to do always what is right in your sight and to avoid that which is evil.

Imbue us with that noble aspiration that the glory of your holy name should come first and foremost in our life, and give us the grace to have a strong determination to accomplish it willingly and cheerfully.

Enable us to attain this kind of determination and give us the courage and tact to influence and persuade others to do likewise.

Help us never to fail in our determination to bring glory and honour to your name, always and everywhere.

QUOTATION

Strength comes not from physical capacity. It comes from an indomitable will.

(Mahatma Gandhi)

38

GENEROSITY

ANECDOTE: "PLEASE, GIVE ME YOUR FANS!"

It happened that an artist visited the home of two little twin girls who were celebrating their birthday.

As one of their gifts, each of them received a fan.

In a friendly but impressive manner, the artist requested them to give him the fans.

One of the girls gave it willingly to him, the other turned away saying impudently: "It was given to me and I want to keep it."

Few days later the artist came back to that home and returned the fan to the girl but with a beautiful picture on it that had increased its value a thousand fold. The girl was overwhelmed with joy. The other girl sulked with remorse.

THOUGHT

The generosity of the girl in giving the fan to the artist was the cause of a greater generosity of the artist towards her.

After sharing our gifts with others, we learn that major benefits have come to ourselves as well, because one of our deepest joys in life is to know that we have brought some happiness to those whose life we have been privileged to enrich. Besides, sharing our gifts with others produces a strong effect on our own happiness and a sense of fulfilment. It generates not only meaning to the present, but also hope for our future, in the sense that if we have shared them with others, we shall not stand empty handed before God.

Let us acknowledge that whatever gifts we have in our lives, are given to us not just for ourselves, but for the sake of others as well. Keeping our gifts and talents for ourselves only, may tend to lose their meaning.

PRAYER

O Lord God, thank you for all the beautiful things you have given to us, and for all the kindness we have received from others.

We ask pardon for the times when we did not share our blessings with others or returned the kindness given to us.

We want to assure you that from today onwards we shall be more kind-hearted and generous by sharing with others the gifts that we receive.

QUOTATION

There is more happiness in giving than in receiving.

(Acts 20:35)

39

COURAGE

ANECDOTE: A REMARKABLE WOMAN

A telephone operator was warned by a resident of the hills to flee for her life because a flood was speeding to engulf the valley.

But she preferred saving others' lives than her own. In fact she employed her time in calling up subscribers, one after the other, informing them of the imminent danger.

More than forty families acknowledged their lives saved through the magnificent courage of one frail woman who was not afraid to lose her life by drowning to save theirs.

Her lifeless body, with the telephone headpiece still adjusted to her ears, was found fifteen kilometres down the canyon.

THOUGHT

Courage is that ability to defend unflinchingly those principles and those values that a person holds dear, even in the face of death.

The principal act of courage is to endure and to

withstand dangers bravely, rather than to attack them.

It does not stem from the absence of fear, but from the capability of facing it.

Courage is inherently dynamic.

PRAYER

O Lord God, endow us with the courage to walk every step of our life with great faith and trust in you knowing that your light may be our guide, that your presence may be our defence, and that your love may be our strength and inspiration.

Give us the courage to do the good things we are afraid to do, and that we may bring courage to those others who want to do the right thing and are finding it difficult to accomplish it.

Endow us with courage and strength to avoid all evil, and at the same time to be a source of courage and strength to those who want to imitate us.

QUOTATION

The greatest test of courage on earth is to face adversity without losing heart.

(R.G. Ignersoll)

40

TIME SO PRECIOUS

ANECDOTE: WORLD'S OLDEST WOMAN DIES

A woman, proclaimed the world's oldest person for April 1998, died peacefully when she was 117 years of age.

She lived 7 months beyond her 117th birthday. "I can confirm that she died peacefully of natural causes, in the afternoon," a nurse at the home said.

She was born on August 29, 1880. She was deemed the world's oldest person by the Guinness Book of Records.

THOUGHT

There is no doubt that the most precious possession we have is time. We all possess it in a limited quantity. How much we have is known to God alone. Some of us have a long period of time to live, others a short one. But whether it is long or short, we know by our own experience that it flies, and it flies fast, never to return.

Time cannot be bought or sold, it cannot be transferred, it cannot be hastened on or slowed down. It is not in our hands, it is in God's hands.

Let us for a moment reflect how we have used our

time so far, how we are using it at present, and how we intend using it in the future.

PRAYER

O Lord God, we acknowledge you as the maker of time and of us, give us the strength and the sense to waste not even a little bit of it at all.

We want to thank you for the help you have given us in using it well, with profit for ourselves and for others.

We regret and are sorry for the time we have squandered and wasted, and ask you to pardon us for doing so.

We are determined with the help of your grace to use our time better in the future and to put in good use every moment of it.

QUOTATION

Dost thou love life? Then do not squander time, for that's the stuff life is made of.

(Benjamin Franklin)

41

RUINING OUR LIFE

ANECDOTE: FORCING THE BUD TO OPEN

A girl went to a florist to buy a red rose to give it to her mother as a birthday present. In the shop there was not a single rose that was fully opened, there were only buds. With a look of disgust she bought the largest bud.

On her way home she tried to force it open with the result that she completely ruined the budding rose.

What would have become a beautiful large red rose was simply a mashed mess of half-formed petals in her hands.

She didn't give it to her mother, as it was such a disgrace even to show it to her.

THOUGHT

Every thing in nature blooms in its own time. We, human beings are not an exception.

There was a time when all of us were children, now we are grown-ups. That did not happen in an instant. It took us years to change. We are still growing and maturing, but we do not know for how long, since we do not know how long we are going to live. That is known to God alone.

Hence it behoves us to make the best of the time we have right now at our disposal, conscious of the fact that every moment is invaluable. Let us strive to keep on changing for the better.

Prayer

O Lord God, help us to live our life to the full, but without expecting more than what can be given, without risking the danger of forcing what should not be forced. We know that you do not expect of us more than what we are able to give.

Help us to learn our own limitations, our shortcomings, our defects and our sins. In like manner let us not expect from others more than they are able to give.

Be with us always that we may not ruin our life, but to return it to you as beautiful as you would expect to have it back from us.

Quotation

If you deliberately jump into a well, providence is not bound to fetch you out.

(Thomas Fullern)

42

OUR NEIGHBOUR

ANECDOTE: THE PILOT AND THE DRIVER

One evening, a pilot was flying his single-engine aeroplane towards a small country airport. Before he could get the plane into position to land, dusk fell and he could not see the hazy field below. He had no lights on his plane and there was no one on duty at the airport. After circling for two hours, when by then the darkness had deepened and the plane's fuel was almost expended, he decided to try a crash landing, which would have probably meant his death.

At that moment, a driver passing close to the airstrip heard the engine of the plane and noticing the total darkness at the airport realised the plight of the pilot. He took action immediately by driving his car back and forth on the runway to show where the airstrip was positioned and then shone the headlights from the far end of the strip to guide the pilot to a safe landing.

THOUGHT

The driver helped the pilot out of his grave predicament not because they were friends, actually they did not know each other at all, but because the pilot was his neighbour in great need of help.

No doubt, friends must help friends, but help should not be limited only between friends. We must help our neighbour whoever he or she may be.

The roads of life, no matter where we live, have neighbours lying helpless by the wayside, and to such we must offer our help.

PRAYER

O Lord God, do not tolerate us to shut our eyes or turn a deaf ear when we come across any person waiting and hoping that someone will come along to offer a helping hand.

Make us show interest and actually give help to anybody needing help and assistance in corporal, mental or spiritual needs.

Help us to help, not only when it is pleasant to help, but also when it is difficult to give help and when we do not feel like giving it.

QUOTATION

Do nothing to your neighbour which you would not hereafter have your neighbour do to you. You obtain a rule of action by looking upon your neighbour like yourself.

(Mahabharata)

43

OUR CONSCIENCE

ANECDOTE: HOUNDED BY HER CONSCIENCE

A 25-year-old woman went about for three years before confessing that she had committed a murder. With every probability the police would never have implicated her.

To keep her crime from being discovered she had more than the police to deal with. She was continuously pursued and hounded everywhere she went by her own conscience.

Unable to stand the pangs any longer she gave up herself to the police and admitted that she had poisoned her roommate. The authorities had long before pronounced the roommate dead of natural causes.

She confessed that her roommate had asked her to move out of the house but she refused to comply and that was why she had murdered her.

THOUGHT

The conscience is that message by which God communicates to us his findings within us. Through it God tells us how we stand before him. It urges us to relinquish what is evil and return to what is good.

Through our conscience God invites us to a harmony with himself, and when we respond favourably, we experience the saving power of the infinite love that He has for each and every one of us.

Conscience has an extraordinary power. This is especially true when any of God's commandments is implied.

PRAYER

O Lord God, when we feel our conscience pricking us, may we understand immediately that it is not a sign that you are rebuking us, but that you are lovingly and patiently calling us back to you.

May we never stifle our conscience especially when we realise that it is urging us to lift up ourselves from the mire of evil.

Help us to comprehend that our conscience is that power of your love working within us seeking to heal us and to free us from evil.

QUOTATION

The testimony of a good conscience is the glory of a good person; have a good conscience and you will ever have gladness.

(Thomas a Kempis)

44

KINDNESS

ANECDOTE: PAID IN FULL

After a successful operation the surgeon smiled at the frail lady and told her: "You've done it, my dear! Within this week you can go home."

"I didn't do it, Doctor," she answered, "It was your skill, and your great kindness!" She paused and then continued: "Your bills are always so small, Doctor, and I even have to remind you to send them. I'm not rich, but I wish to pay. Please do let me know what I owe you. I'm very grateful to you."

The surgeon nodded briskly and said: "You'll hear from me very soon."

Few days later, the lady received her bill. The figure was shockingly large for her to pay. But at the bottom of the sheet, in the doctor's own handwriting were the words: "Paid in full with a gracious personality."

THOUGHT

The doctor and his patient were two persons who showed kindness to each other but completely in a different way, the doctor through his professional work and the lady by her words of praise and appreciation.

Kindness is that disposition showing friendliness, affection or consideration towards others.

Let us remember that every day we have numerous opportunities of being kind to others. We daily meet people who can best be helped by a little bit of kindness, a thoughtful and loving consideration, often because of their problems.

PRAYER

O Lord God, endow our hearts with kindliness so that we may miss no opportunity to cheer, to comfort, to encourage, to praise and to help others especially those who have been kind to us. Let us return kindness with greater kindness if possible.

In our dealings with others make us always courteous and kind in our words, gestures and actions.

We shall strive that every word we speak and every deed we do will be pleasing to you in so far as they do some good to others.

We ask you to pardon us if ever we have failed to do so.

QUOTATION

If there is any good that I can do or any kindness that I can show, let me do it quickly, for I shall not pass this way again.

(Phillips Brooks)

45

DURING DARK MOMENTS

ANECDOTE: AFTER WINTER SPRING COMES

It was on the 21st of March when early in the morning, a little girl, after getting up from her sleep, went running to her mother and quite excitedly told her: "Mom, today is the first day of spring, so the teacher told us, and yesterday was the last day of winter."

"That's true," her mother agreed, "winter with its cold and gloomy days has passed. Spring brings with it sunny days that will invite us to go for walks in the countryside to enjoy the beautiful flowers in the fields and to listen to the babbling brooks and the singing of the birds and to watch with awe the colourful sunsets that decorate the skies beyond our imagination."

THOUGHT

If ever in our life we pass through the darker hours, as most probably every one of us will sooner or later experience, for a short time or for a long time, let us keep in mind that after the winter spring follows, and that the sun shines brightly after the rain.

There is a proverb that says: "After bad weather

comes fine weather", and another one says, "So goes the world, now woe, now weal."

When passing through difficult times we must not lose heart or despair.

PRAYER

O Lord God, when we have to face difficult times, let your Spirit speak to our mind and to our heart so that we will have the power to overcome them, and to look forward with optimism.

Let us never give in to negative thinking; that will only make our burdens heavier. Let us instead concentrate ourselves on changing for the better whatever we can.

We thank you for the temptations and difficulties we have overcome; for the new and important experiences we have learnt; and for the good and useful things we have done.

QUOTATION

There is something infinitely healing in these repeated refrains of nature, the assurance that after night, dawn comes, and spring after winter.

(Rachel Carson)

46

OUR MISTAKES

ANECDOTE: IT PLUNGED INTO THE MOUNTAIN

A Boeing 727-200 slammed into a mountainside, killing all 53 people on board. It crashed shortly after takeoff from the city's airport.

The plane, which belonged to the military, was believed to be travelling at about 200 km per hour when it strayed mysteriously off its assigned flight path and plunged into the mountain.

It careened into the mountain with such a force that the debris from it showered down on a far away residential area of the city, and its three engines plunged down a deep canyon.

Intensive investigations were launched to determine what had gone wrong.

THOUGHT

These investigations were held not only to determine the cause of the accident but more so to learn how to avoid the occurrence of such accidents. The lessons learned might save many lives in the future.

In our lives too we can learn from our mistakes, if

only we determine to put aside some time in which we can examine ourselves and detect how they had happened and what can be done to avoid them in the future.

In fact we can even turn a mistake, an adversity, even a tragedy, into our benefit. No doubt, we can learn from them to become better persons.

PRAYER

O Lord God, may we never commit any mistakes at all, but we know that due to our frailty we are going to make mistakes now and then, perhaps even grave ones.

Inspire us to examine ourselves rigorously so that we may learn not only to avoid doing the same mistakes but also to strengthen ourselves against all evil.

Move us to examine our actions daily that we may put right the wrong we do during the day and make better the good we perform the day after.

QUOTATION

A man may make a mistake; none but a fool will stick to it.

To stumble twice against the same stone is a proverbial disgrace.

(Cicero)

47

LISTENING

ANECDOTE: WHAT DO WE HEAR?

One day, a man who was very fond of his dog had the mishap of a lifetime. His children left the door of the house open, and the dog went out and did not come back.

When the man returned from work and learned what had happened, he left home immediately searching for it, both with his eyes as well as with his ears.

In spite of the din of the traffic and the sounds of the people all around, he detected the feeble barking of his dog coming from a distance.

He managed to locate it, and found his dog in a deep ditch into which it had fallen and from where it could not come out by itself.

THOUGHT

We hear what we listen for. The truth of this statement is evident. Take, for instance, the players in a football match, they recognise the whistle of the referee while blocking out all the noise being done by the supporters, spectators and the crowd in general.

It is imperative in life to be good listeners. Of course,

we must be able to judge who is worth listening to and who is not, and to discern what is worth listening to, and what is not.

This discernment to choose who and what to listen to is of the utmost importance in our lives.

PRAYER

O Lord God, help us to be good listeners. Above all let us listen attentively to your voice by which you speak to us in many different ways. We know that you can speak and reveal yourself to us from outside us as well as from inside us.

May we be humble enough so as to heed and to act on what your mysterious words speak to us.

We want to thank you for deigning to speak to us and we ask you to forgive us when we did not care to listen.

QUOTATION

Listen to yourself, listen to God, when you have led yourself to him. Listen, well, for if you hear his voice you will be wise with the wisdom of God.

(Catherine de Hueck Doherty)

48

TAKING RISKS

ANECDOTE: A STABBING SCENE

The audience went into a delirium, cheering and applauding with great fervour. On the stage the famous actor groaning, staggered into the wings.

"We have never seen a stabbing scene so perfectly done," people in the audience were telling each other. Little did they realise how realistic the scene had been.

The actor was immediately rushed to the hospital with a six centimetres of cold steel in his stomach, as his collapsible dagger had failed to collapse.

THOUGHT

Life is full of risks. We may even say that life is one long risk, from the moment of our birth up to our death. Anything can happen at any time, and often does.

As we go through life we have to take risks. Taking risks is often necessary, and no doubt, when we take a risk we are liable to make a mistake. However if a risk is to be taken we should not fear, we must take it. But we must be very cautious.

In that case we should not rely and depend solely on

ourselves, we must have recourse to God for his help and guidance.

PRAYER

O Lord God, we fully know that without calculated risks, our life would be absolutely dull, boring, uninteresting, stagnant and not worth living at all.

When we have to take a risk, even such a small one as crossing a busy road, help us not only to be cautious and in full control of ourselves, but also to be aware of your guidance and of your deep concern for each moment of our lives.

We are very confident that with the aid of your guidance we can overcome every obstacle that crosses our way.

Help us not to be afraid of taking appropriate risks so that we might actualise the full potentials of our lives.

QUOTATION

The risk must be taken, because the greater hazard in life is to risk nothing. The person who risks nothing, does nothing, has nothing and is nothing.

(Daniel P. Cronin)

49

PRAISING OTHERS

ANECDOTE: A SINCERE COMPLIMENT

It was the annual sports day of the school. Two students from the same class were taking part in the same 100 metre race.

One of them was regarded as the favourite to win the event, yet it was not he who had won it but the other one. It was the other one who actually touched the line first.

The loser like a good sportsman was quick to approach the winner and wholeheartedly complimented him. He hugged him and told him: "Congratulations! You deserve it. You did better."

THOUGHT

By praising someone or something we express our approval, satisfaction, admiration and appreciation for their achievements or qualities.

A compliment is an expression of praise.

By praising others we approve and affirm the good they do. Moreover we instil courage in them and stimulate them to continue striving hard to better the good they do.

When we praise God, we express our respect, honour and thanks to him.

PRAYER

O Lord God, help us to be quick to praise where praise is due. Let us not hesitate or feel reluctant to compliment, to congratulate or to praise others.

Keep us alive that we shall not miss such opportunities to bring happiness in others' hearts.

For the times, and for all the occasions when we could have easily praised others and failed, we are sorry.

Then also, we ask you to help us so that when others praise us, we will not let it go to our heads but rather to accept it modestly.

QUOTATION

Help us at all times, O God, to encourage and not to dishearten, to be more ready to praise than to condemn, to uplift rather than to disparage, to hide rather than to expose the faults of others.

(T. Glyn Thomas)

50

FLATTERY

ANECDOTE: SHE WAS SHOCKED

A young lady used to go to the hospital to visit her 80-year-old grandfather.

One day when she approached his bed, she was appalled by the look on his face. The man's eyes were turned up, his tongue was stuck out and his face wearing an ugly grimace.

Shocked as she was, the young lady uttered: "What has happened to your face? You look terrible!"

Suddenly her grandfather changed his face into a lovely smile and said: "My dear girl, I'm tired of people telling me how well I look. So I've decided to do something that would make the next visitor tell me frankly how horrible I look. And, by Jove, I've succeeded!"

THOUGHT

Flattery is pleasing only to fools. We should not make the mistake in confusing well-chosen and tactful compliments with mean flattery.

There is a vast difference between praise and flattery. The former is founded on truth and reality, the latter is based on hypocrisy and insincerity. Hence, the one is honest, the other is dishonest.

It is not only uncharitable to flatter but it is also unjust.

Usually flattery does a lot of harm not only to the one who accepts it but also to the one who addresses it.

Often flattery is also used to please or to persuade someone to do something, which one was unwilling or reluctant to do.

PRAYER

O Lord God, we understand that a thoughtful and judicious compliment gives not only pleasure but also encouragement. For this reason we ask you to help us trying to find in others the qualities on which they may deservedly be congratulated.

Help us to encourage others without ever flattering them. Make us realise that by praising others we help them to grow, but by flattering them they may retard or even stop altogether to make any effort to improve.

QUOTATION

He that slanders me paints me blacker than I am, and he that flatters me, whiter. They both daub me, and when I look in the glass of conscience, I see myself disguised by both.

(William Cowper)

51

MAGNANIMITY

ANECDOTE: AN OX AND A YOUNG MAN

A story is narrated of a traveller, who while passing through a village, came upon an old man ploughing his field with an old plough that was being drawn by an ox and a young man harnessed together.

Full of astonishment he asked the old man for the queer reason. The answer was that the people of the village had decided to build a place of worship but the funds collected for the purpose were not enough. So the old man's son suggested that since they had nothing to give they would sell one of their two oxen, give the proceeds to the fund, whilst he himself would take the yoke of the ox. That is what they did.

THOUGHT

In these days there are so many worthy charities and funds to give to. It is only meet that we ask ourselves: "When have we last been generous with any such like organisations truly deserving our help?"

'Give until it hurts,' the saying goes. How many of us actually do so? Such persons are very few, and most

probably we are not included amongst them. The young man and his father were among the few; in giving they were being hurt very deeply. However, with every probability, they were also experiencing in their hearts the great joy of such giving.

PRAYER

O Lord God, help us to have not mere sympathy towards others but to show compassion in action by being generous. Teach us to give often and generously.

Give us the courage to be able to spend not merely the money that we have, but our own very life for you and your people.

We know that when we die you will not express your gratitude for the possessions we will have amassed, but you will thank us for the amount we will have given to others who were in dire need of it.

QUOTATION

**Lord, give my eyes the gift to see the other person's need,
And take from me my selfishness, self-centredness and greed,
And make my ears attentive to the hard cry of despair.
Lord, grant that I will go without while others have my share.**

(Bernard Boon)

52

NEVER GIVE IN

ANECDOTE: THE TWO DOGS

Two dogs were playing by running one after the other. This chasing took them to a pit of dirty water where they fell, causing them to struggle frantically to get out and save themselves.

Finally, after trying hard for a long time without success, one of them uttered in despair: "I give up!" Soon it went under the water and was drowned.

The other dog was determined not to give up. He kept himself floating and barking every now and then.

A man who was passing by heard the barking and when he saw the dog struggling in the hole, he pulled it out and saved it.

THOUGHT

We are sometimes afraid to tackle certain demands of life because they seem to be too difficult for us to attain, for instance in regaining good health, or in securing a good place in society, or in studies, or in achieving an aim. It often seems to be so much easier to just give in rather than to struggle.

We will succeed only if we keep on trying, even though we may think that there "isn't a chance in a million", there may be one chance we don't see. But if we stop trying, there will surely be no chance at all. We admit that we are defeated.

PRAYER

O Lord God, in difficult times, when we feel that the burden is too heavy to carry, we are tempted to give in. We may say to ourselves that there is no hope, no chance, no use. Make us realise then that what is impossible for us human beings, it is quite possible for you. Teach us to turn to you, you who are able to do what we cannot do.

At those moments when we feel that we are going to be crashed under our own problems, due to the lack of determination with which we face them and also because of the little trust, if at all, we place in you, come to our aid by strengthening our will not to give in, and by increasing our trust in you.

QUOTATION

Never give in! Never give in! Never, never, never, never, never, – in anything great or small, large or petty – never give in except to convictions of honour and good sense.

(Winston Churchill)

53

SYMPATHY

ANECDOTE: A FARMER, HIS WIFE AND THE MULE

A traveller, while on a mountain trail, met a farmer riding on a mule, with his wife walking behind him.

The traveller stopped and in a tone of great surprise he asked the farmer: "Why isn't your wife riding?"

The farmer was quick to reply: "Because she has no mule, and this one is not hers."

THOUGHT

Can we say that the farmer was feeling sorry for his wife? Who knows! Perhaps he was in his own way! He might have thought to himself: "It's too bad that my wife has to walk! If only she had a mule of her own!"

Undoubtedly there are many of us who resemble the farmer in our attitude towards others. How often we ourselves do as he had done! How often we say that we are sorry for those in need, but then under some pretext or another we fail to help, even though we may have all the means at our disposal whereby we could relieve their burden.

PRAYER

O Lord God, you know that there were times when we had expressed our sympathy and felt sorry for those who were in dire need of our assistance, but we failed to actually help them.

Forgive us for those occasions when we merely showed our sympathy only in words without converting it, as we should, into action.

Forgive us when in spite of the abundance of the things we possessed we did not care to give even a little bit to those in need whereby we could have relieved their hardship.

Whenever we find ourselves in such unpleasant and pitiful circumstances open our minds to discern what we ought to do, and more so, touch our hearts to follow the way in which we can do it.

QUOTATION

**Per chance a look will suffice to clear
    the cloud from a neighbour's face,
And the press of a hand in sympathy
    a sorrowful tear efface.**

(Anon)

54

RETALIATION

ANECDOTE: VICTIM OF HIS OWN TRAP

A man tried to protect his summer residence during the wintertime by installing a .22-calibre rifle in such a way that if anybody opened the door, it would automatically fire at the intruder.

On returning the following summer, the man found the windows had been smashed. Thinking that once again some robber had broken in, he rushed to the door quite unaware of the impending danger. As soon as he stepped inside the room, his own booby trap went off and hit him in the chest.

He managed to crawl to the road close by where a passing motorist picked him up and rushed him to a hospital in a critical condition.

THOUGHT

When others harm or annoy us, and we do something to harm or annoy them in return, that is retaliation.

It is very natural that we do not like to be robbed of our possessions. We protect them as best as we can. In fact we use safes, strongboxes, chests, and the like.

However, we can overdo things, as for example, when we become too enraged, hard-hearted, vindictive.

There are times when we become so preoccupied about the safety of our life and of our possessions that we exaggerate to the limit the safeguards and the precautions that we take.

PRAYER

O Lord God, when others do us any harm, however grave it may be, help us to deal with them, if deal we must, not with excessive anger and revenge, but rather reasonably and with consideration.

Help us to understand that we should not do an ill turn to another if we do not want it to be done to ourselves. Let us realise that the evil we try to do to others may backfire and we ourselves become the victims of our own misdeed.

We ask pardon for those times when we had taken the law into our hands, retaliated, avenged ourselves, or were vindictive. May we never again have recourse to such evil doing.

QUOTATION

The man who sets a trap for others will get caught in it himself. Roll a boulder down on someone, and it will roll back and crush you.

(Proverbs 26:27)

55

PESSIMISM

ANECDOTE: THE TWO BUCKETS

Two buckets in a well were connected to each other by a rope which passed over a pulley, so that when one immersed into the water, the other rose up.

One of them was always worried and sad, complaining that however full he came up he always went down empty.

The other one was always cheerful and elated that however empty he went down he always came up full to the brim.

THOUGHT

A pessimist is one who tends to take the worst view, or expects the worst outcome of everything, for no valid reason whatsoever.

Such a one is often a worried person, wasting countless hours being sad without experiencing a little bit of happiness.

We should not waste our valuable time and energy in distress and anxiety, worrying and fretting about things that cannot be changed or that, after all, they may never happen.

If we want to live a happy and cheerful life let us always endeavour to look at the bright side of things.

PRAYER

O Lord God, help us so that we will not fall into the very bad habit of taking a gloomy and despondent view of things.

Help us to be always among those people who praise you for putting roses among thorns, and never to be among those who complain that you put thorns on roses.

Make us ever conscious that you are actually on our side, and always near. This thought of your guiding presence will undoubtedly deepen our awareness that at the end of the dark tunnel we shall come out into the bright light.

QUOTATION

The pessimist sees difficulty in every opportunity, the optimist an opportunity in every difficulty.

(L.P. Jacks)

56

GIVING

ANECDOTE: THE PIG AND THE COW

In a friendly conversation between a pig and a cow, the pig lamented about the lack of popularity he enjoyed among the people.

"You cows are liked by the people much more than we pigs are. This is so in spite of giving them more than you give them. You give them milk and cream while we give them bacon and ham and bristles for brushes," the pig complained.

The cow listened attentively, and after thinking for a little while, she remarked: "People like us more than they like you, very probably because what we give, is given during our lifetime; you give only after you are dead."

THOUGHT

There are many ways in which we may give. We may give because it is our duty to comply, or because we cannot do otherwise, or out of contempt, or to make a show, or for the pleasure of being thanked, and so on.

But we may also give as a sign of joy and pleasure,

120

moved by our concern, care and love for others. Most probably this brings even more gladness to those who give rather than to those who receive.

After all, God loves a cheerful giver.

PRAYER

O Lord God, help us to realise that we should not give for the sake of bringing happiness to ourselves, to be praised, to be popular or to be thanked. But let us give with the intention of doing good to others, to make them happy, to alleviate their suffering, to lift them up from their poverty and misery, for a good cause.

Open wide our eyes to see the needs of others less fortunate than ourselves, and then, when we decide to give, let us give immediately, without hesitation or delay, keeping in mind that tomorrow may never come.

May we keep in mind the saying: He gives twice who gives quickly.

QUOTATION

The truth is that human beings are only at peace with themselves and therefore contented when they feel that they are giving more than they are taking, not because they are compelled to give, but because they want to.

(Sir Arthur Bryant)

57

DEPENDENCY

ANECDOTE: A MOTHER'S ONLY WISH

A mother received the very sad news that her soldier son had fallen fighting bravely in battle.

Inconsolable as she was, she prayed: "Oh, if I could see him again, even if only for five minutes!"

Instantly she heard a voice telling her: "Yes, your wish is granted, but how would you like to see him in his life of thirty years? Would you see him as a soldier dying heroically on the front? Would you see him on his first day at school? Would you see him receiving the highest honours as a student in his college? How?"

With her eyes full of tears she answered: "I would like to see him as on that day when as a little child he ran into my arms telling me: 'Mummy, I need you. Pardon me for being naughty. I love you so much!'"

THOUGHT

The one thing that the good mother wished to recall to her mind and to see again, was an episode when her son needed her.

A person may have no lovelier feeling than to be

needed. It is so moving to hear the words 'I need you; I cannot do without you.'

It is a very satisfying feeling to know that we had aided someone, even if in a small way, to attain success in something or another.

PRAYER

O Lord God, help us that while we strive hard to be able to stand on our own two feet and to meet life boldly as it comes to us, let us understand that we depend so much on others, and especially on you.

We want to confess to you, that we would rather travel with you in the dark than go it all alone in the light, because we know fully well that without you we can do nothing.

We are confident that nothing can happen to us that you and we cannot handle together.

May we never forget what we owe to you and to those who have helped us to be who we are. May we be grateful for all the support we still receive.

QUOTATION

Pray to God as if everything depends on him; work as if everything depends on you.

(Cardinal Spellman)

58

FORGIVING OUR ENEMIES

ANECDOTE: A SOLDIER'S LETTER

During the Second World War, a soldier wrote to a mother: "While my Commando Unit was raiding a village, it became unavoidable for me to kill your son who came face to face with me in combat. I earnestly beg your forgiveness... I hope that some day after the war is over, I may come to talk with you in person."

Receiving the letter several months later, the mother wrote back: "I do forgive you wholeheartedly, yes, you who killed my son... If we are still living after the war is over, do please come to visit me, that you may, even though for a short time, take the place of my son in my home. I assure you that I still cherish his memory with great affection."

THOUGHT

In granting forgiveness to the soldier who had killed her son, the mother had shown great understanding and compassion.

At the same time, the soldier writing the letter to the

sorrowful mother asking her to forgive him, must have exercised great humility and courage.

All of us are very frail, and we often fail one another. There are times when we hurt one another even in a big way.

True forgiveness, both in asking and in giving, is always an act of the free will. It removes the feeling of resentment and animosity.

Actually forgiveness is the very first step towards love.

PRAYER

O Lord God, we confess that asking for forgiveness for ourselves or to grant forgiveness to others, does not come easily to us, it is rather very difficult.

We earnestly pray that if ever the need arises, do help us to break the hard shell enclosing our proud and haughty heart, so that we will humble enough ourselves so as to ask for pardon, or again that we may willingly pardon others their offences against us.

Deepen our faith in your compassionate forgiveness.

QUOTATION

Better by far that you should forgive and smile than that you should remember and be sad.

(Christina Rossetti)

59

THANKS

ANECDOTE: THE STUDENT AND HIS TEACHER

A student asked the teacher to allow him to leave the classroom because within a few minutes' time his father would come to pick him up to take him to the hospital for a medical check up.

The teacher, after consulting the letter addressed to him by the student's father, immediately granted the permission.

The student put all his books and other things in the satchel and hurriedly walked to the door.

As he was going out, he heard the teacher telling him: "May I please remind you to say 'thank you'!"

THOUGHT

The student did not say 'thank you', probably because it skipped his mind due to his preoccupation that he was going to the hospital. Such things do happen to most of us.

But there are times when we take things for granted and do not bother to say 'thanks'. That can be real thoughtlessness, inconsideration, lack of appreciation, and sometimes even ingratitude.

Let us ask the question to ourselves: "Are we truly thankful for the favours we receive, or do we let them go by as if nothing has happened?"

It would be a shame on our part if on receiving a benefit we do not acknowledge it with thanks.

PRAYER

O Lord God, we ask for the awareness to appreciate the benefits that we receive. How many people have been so good to us in the past, and how many others are still so kind to us at present!

May we never lose the memory of the favours we receive, which should remain fresh in our minds, so that we may always show our appreciation, and give thanks.

Keep reminding us that on receiving a benefit it is our indispensable duty to say 'thanks' in order to show that we value it.

QUOTATION

Who does not thank for little, will not thank for much.

(Estonian Proverb)

60

RIGHT AND WRONG

The manager of a supermarket was just saying how annoyed he was by the continual round of complaints being received from shoppers on that busy day. He lamented: "Every hour someone or other has found fault with the service, the goods, the lack of courtesy from the sales persons or with something else."

He had hardly finished the sentence when he heard the telephone ringing again.

Taking up the receiver he heard a woman's voice telling him: "I'm just phoning to tell you how much I enjoyed my shopping at your store this morning. In particular the sales girls whom I have found very helpful were also so courteous."

THOUGHT

Many are those people who keep harping on what is wrong around them, as if there is not a little bit of good. Such people seem to take pleasure in finding faults, criticising and condemning.

These days we need to have more people to point out

what is good and right with the world, and less to trumpet what is wrong with it.

To show that we are included into this blissful category of people who appreciate that there is so much good in the world, let us make it a point to praise someone today for the good he or she has done.

PRAYER

O Lord God, help us to spend more time manifesting the good that we notice, rather than in complaining about what is wrong.

May we be more attentive to the signs of goodness in the people and things around us, rather than pinpointing the evil we may detect in them.

Help us to cultivate our positive attitudes towards life that we may enjoy its goodness, and deepen our awareness of the beauty and splendour with which we are surrounded.

Help us to be always inclined to point out what is right rather than what is wrong.

QUOTATION

Two men look out through the same bars of the same window in their cell; one sees only the mud, and the other sees the stars.

(F. Landridge)

61

DOING OUR PART

ANECDOTE: A BOY AND HIS BIRD'S TRAP

One morning an eleven-year-old boy set up a trap in their garden to catch sparrows. His younger sister felt very sad about it and ran to her mother accusing him of his cruelty towards these little harmless creatures.

In the afternoon the girl appeared very cheerful and happy. Rather puzzled, her mother inquired into the reason of this sudden change.

"I prayed for brother to become a better boy, and that the trap would not catch any birds," said the girl, for which her mother praised her.

"And then," continued the girl, "I went to the trap and with a big stone I broke it to pieces."

THOUGHT

Undoubtedly it is very good to pray so that wrongs will be righted, but we should not be satisfied with just praying. We must also do our part as best as we can to make them right.

There is a saying that goes: 'Prayer and work go hand in hand'. The girl has put this axiom into action.

130

Once we pray to God and do whatever we possibly can, then we may trustfully leave every thing in his hands and let him finish the job himself.

PRAYER

O Lord God, we are very confident that when we turn to you in prayer and at the same time we do what is humanly possible to rectify what is wrong, or to make good what is bad, then you will do what we cannot.

We know that you unfailingly help those who earnestly help themselves.

We are aware that we should pray to you in such a way as if what we are praying for depends entirely on you; and at the same time we are convinced that you expect us to act in such a way, as if everything depends solely on us.

We know fully well that what we cannot do, we cannot do, and calmly turn to you in prayer; but what we can, we must do, and do it wholeheartedly.

QUOTATION

Pray to God, but row for the shore.

(Russian Proverb)

62

ENCOURAGEMENT

ANECDOTE: A MEDAL FOR THE MAN

It was wintertime and the sea was rather rough. A young girl fell into the sea and was drowning. Her companions began calling for help.

A man passing by, realising what was happening, removed his coat and shoes, leapt into the sea, and after some struggle saved her.

Moved by gratitude, the girl's father praised the man in all the local newspapers, and tried to get a medal for him from the civil authority. This caused the police to look up the man's records and found out that he did have trouble with them for creating public disturbances due to fighting.

All the same the award was given to him for his bravery in risking his life to save that of another.

It is said that after receiving the award he reformed himself and never again had any trouble with the police. Moreover he had even joined an association for doing voluntarily charitable works.

THOUGHT

As in this case, an act of generosity may start off a wrong doer on a new path that may change his or her life.

An act of kindness, a word of encouragement, a gesture of confidence, a sign of assurance or even a loving smile by us may cause the difference between hope and despair, joy and sadness, to many a person in trouble.

There is criticism enough in the world, let us try some encouragement instead.

PRAYER

O Lord God, help us to encourage and not to dishearten, to be more ready to praise than to condemn.

Make us realise that a word of encouragement can be of infinite value to the person concerned, because as we ourselves might have experienced, the feeling that someone is urging us on to achievement, is one of the very pleasant feelings in life.

Let us never fail to see and encourage the good in others, knowing that there is nothing in the world which will pull out a person as encouragement will.

QUOTATION

Our chief want in life is somebody who shall make us do what we can.

(Ralph Waldo)

63

HASTE

ANECDOTE: THE COMMANDING OFFICER

A commanding officer lined up some of his best soldiers to ask for volunteers among them for a very perilous mission.

He first explained the risks involved. Then he told them that if there was anyone willing to volunteer for the task to take two paces forward.

At that precise moment a subordinate officer approached him and handed to him an urgent message.

When he turned back to his men, seeing the line still unbroken, he felt so disconcerted and angry that he yelled: "What a shame! Not a single one has come forward!"

It did not take him long to realise that he was too hasty in his judgement as he soon noticed that the entire line had advanced the two paces.

THOUGHT

Experience teaches us that actions taken without sufficient reflection are often mistaken, and hasty decisions are generally wrong.

So also we should not do anything in a hurry if we

want to do things well, because work done hastily is often done very badly.

Haste makes for confusion.

Moreover work done in haste, besides being generally bad, is also a waste of time, energy and money.

PRAYER

O Lord God, we are often like that Commanding officer in the sense that we are also inclined to judge others hastily. But while the Commanding officer had noticed his mistake quite quickly and so no harm was caused, unlike him we may notice our mistake quite late when great harm and injustice might have already been done to others.

Help us that we may never act hastily so that we will not cause any inconvenience to others and perhaps make ourselves sorry about the outcome.

QUOTATION

Haste makes waste.

(English Proverb)

64

CARING

ANECDOTE: THE TWO TRAVELLERS

One bitterly cold day, unremitting snow found two men travelling along on foot to a far off destination.

While struggling hard along the way, they met a man lying in the snow and unable to move on.

One of the two suggested to rescue the poor man, but the other refused to help and walked ahead alone.

With great difficulty, the other traveller managed to get the helpless man on to his back and struggled on his way.

Before long and to his great shock he came upon a dead body; it was that of his companion frozen to death.

THOUGHT

Like the kind-hearted traveller of the story, it often happens that when we care for others, untold blessings enrich our own lives. In his efforts to save the dying man, the traveller had grown warm and while saving the poor man's life, he saved his own.

We show that we care for others not when we try so much to catch their attention on us, but when we give

them our whole attention; so also, not when we expect
others to come to us, but when we go earnestly to them.

Caring for others promotes self-confidence in them
who receive our care, and at the same time it strengthens
our own as well.

PRAYER

O Lord God, touch our hearts that we may always be
compassionate to others. Through your power working
within us strengthen our caring actions towards those
who are poor, those who are anxious or sad, those who
feel unwanted, those who somehow or somewhat need
us.

For so often, we, who pride ourselves on being decent
human beings, ignore those who need us. No, Lord,
never permit that we would succumb to such a mean
behaviour.

QUOTATION

**If I can stop one heart from breaking I shall not live
in vain. If I can ease in one life the aching, or cool one
pain, or help one fainting robin unto his nest again I
shall not live in vain.**

(Emily Dickinson)

65

FEELINGS

ANECDOTE: LOSING HIS RIGHT HAND

An eleven-year-old boy had his right hand amputated due to a serious car accident. He felt so badly about it that he refused to see anyone.

His father told him: "An old friend of mine, a professor teaching at the university, is coming to see you." The child did not budge, and stubbornly answered: "I don't want to see him, or any one else."

But the father brought him in. As the boy looked up, he was taken aback on seeing the professor having an empty sleeve as he too had no right hand.

The professor leaned over to the boy and remarked: "As you can see, I too have no right hand. I lost it when I was just a little boy like you. I very well know how you are feeling!"

THOUGHT

For days together, a feeling of anger, dejection and frustration depressed the boy, but the sight of another person, a professor, who also had only one hand, helped him to change his attitude, reasoning that the professor too knew very well how one feels on losing one's own hand.

In fact the story goes on to say that the child immediately took a liking towards the professor and became very friendly with him. Above all, he got over that feeling of depression.

PRAYER

O Lord God, we know that feelings have immense power over us. Help us to be their masters, and not their slaves.

We seem to imagine that we please you not by our prayers but by how we feel during our prayers, and think we are saints when we feel saints, and sinners when we feel sinners; while probably the very opposite is true.

We know that there are times when we cannot command our feelings, and that other people may have greater control, or more effective influence over them than we have. They are more likely to compel us to weep, to laugh, to love, to hate, than we can force ourselves to do. Strengthen our reason and our will so that we will not be carried away by such feelings.

QUOTATION

Our whole attitude to life, our efforts at improvement, or the ceasing of all effort, are unfortunately very largely affected by our feelings.

(Bede Jarrett)

66

MONEY

ANECDOTE: DECIDED TO BREAK THE VASE

One day, a little boy who knew that his mother was saving some money in a costly vase, decided to put his hand into it to steal a coin or two.

Then, all efforts to get his hand out of the vase were to no avail. Noticing what was happening his mother came to help him but she too failed to free his hand. His father also came and tried, but he did not succeed either.

After a little while, the parents decided to break the vase, but just before actually breaking it, the father cautioned his son: "Now, son, try for the last time. Pull all your fingers out straight and then make an effort to take your hand out."

At that moment the parents could not believe their ears when they heard the words slip from the mouth of their child: "But then I'll drop the coin!"

THOUGHT

No wonder that the child could not get his hand out of the vase! He was keeping it closed holding a coin tight in it!

The temptation of money can make not only a child, but even the wise among us, to do, say or act foolishly.

He who craves for money often comes to grief on its account because it is the root of all evil, naturally for those who do not make a good use of it.

It has been said that money is the purchaser of anything except death and happiness, and it is a passport to any place except heaven.

PRAYER

O Lord God, we know that you are not against us having money, even lots of it; you are against us misusing it.

Make us realise that money is not everything in life; to be content for instance, is a more important thing. It is a fact that there are poor people in the world who are much more contented than the rich.

Give us enough sense to know how to use our money well, and instil it clearly in our mind that no one died and took any money with him, even millionaires die poor like the poor.

QUOTATION

No man can take his wealth with him to the grave, nor can he escape death by paying a ransom, nor does his hoard of money ward off disease and the approach of age.

(Theocritus)

67

SHARING

ANECDOTE: A BOWL OF RICE

Every day, a woman stood in a line with a bowl in her hand to receive rice for herself and for her four children.

One day, while standing right at the end of the line, another woman carrying a baby and holding a child by the hand, came and stood behind her.

After the first woman received her rations, the newcomer was told that it was all finished. She then asked the woman: "Kindly share yours with me," but she refused, saying: "I need it all for my family," and walked away.

She had not gone far when she stopped and went back to share her rice with the other woman telling her: "Sister, forgive me. Let's share this rice between us. For a moment I had forgotten the Lord."

THOUGHT

To what extent do we share with others from the abundance of our resources? Is it much, little or perhaps nothing at all? Do we just keep everything we have for ourselves only even though we do know that we have exceedingly too much?

Sharing is the ability to enjoy what we possess with others. It is not restricted to material goods. It is the interchange of anything that we may have, the fruit of our brains, the ideas, the warmth of our feelings, our talents, our joys, any thing that is good.

PRAYER

O Lord God, whenever there is anything that others need from us, and we are in a position that we can give it, help us to be very willing to share it with them.

We are often tempted to use our possessions for our own benefit only and to forget that they are meant to be shared. Help us not to yield to this temptation.

Forgive us for not understanding the meaning and the utility of sharing with others whatever we could share, and also for our lack of compassion towards others.

QUOTATION

It is one of the most beautiful compensations of life that no man can sincerely try to help another without helping himself.

(J. Pearson Webster)

68

TEMPTATION

ANECDOTE: ON BUYING A DRESS

A woman went shopping and had spent more money than she could afford. Her main item was an expensive dress.

At home, when her husband showed her his disapproval, she explained: "I couldn't help buying it. The evil one tempted me."

"Why didn't you tell him: 'get behind me, you wretched one?'" her husband asked sharply.

"Oh, that is exactly what I did," the wife promptly replied. "And can you guess what he did? He quickly leaned over my shoulder and whispered in my ear: 'My dear, this dress fits you just beautifully in the back.'"

THOUGHT

The worst thing we can do at the time of temptation is to argue with it. There will be no let-up on its part; it will come up with all sorts of reasons and excuses for us to do the things we know we should not.

If we are enticed to commit evil, we must not consent. Let us remember that temptations do not come that we

may give in to them but that we may prove our worth
against evil. Temptation is always essentially a test.

We should also keep before our eyes that the best way
to avoid evil is to do good.

PRAYER

O Lord God, we know how weak we are and how
dangerous life can be, we humbly ask you to keep us
from flirting with temptation.

Keep us from those occasions in which temptation
will get its chance. Strengthen our will to overcome the
weakness of our own nature, and defend us from the
malice of others so that we will not put ourselves into
life situations in which we are foolishly and needlessly
exposed to temptations.

Defend us from the temptations that the world, the
flesh and the evil one launch against us.

QUOTATION

We cannot help being exposed to temptations, but we
pray not only that we may not fall and perish under
them, but that we should not even enter into the
struggle with them, lest we should fall.

(John Chrysostom)

69

CONCEIT

ANECDOTE: THE ANT AND THE ELEPHANT

One of the ancient fables is about an elephant crossing a bridge with an ant riding on his back.

Because of his heavy weight the elephant made the bridge shake at every step he took while crossing.

When the two reached safely on the other side, the ant proudly exclaimed: "By Jove! We certainly did shake the bridge!"

THOUGHT

A number of us do find the temptation too strong to resist in claiming credit for things that are accomplished with little or no effort on our part. That is what the ant did. It undoubtedly makes us laugh.

It should rather make us sad. Why? Because in doing so we arrogate to ourselves the merit which we know must belong to another. We thereby pretend that it is mainly our own doing.

We swell at the thought of our own importance when we actually do not deserve it.

Conceit, then is not the truth, but a lie. It is the claiming of something which we know is due to another.

PRAYER

O Lord God, make us realise that we should leave the value of our performance to be judged by you and then to give us our due.

We are sure that even if the role we play is small, in your sight it is an important one. You will neither underestimate nor overestimate it. All the same, we are certain that the recompense you make will far outweigh any worldly compensation.

For the number of times we succumbed to our overweening self-esteem and exaggerated high opinion of ourselves, we ask your forgiveness and we promise to be cautious not to fall into the same trap again.

QUOTATION

A fly sat on a chariot wheel and said: "What a dust I raise!"

(La Fontaine)

70

RIGHT ATTITUDE

ANECDOTE: STUDENTS' OBSERVATION POWER

Wishing to test her students' power of observation, a teacher asked them to write down the answer to the question: "What would you think if you went into a room and found cobwebs hanging from the ceiling and on the walls?"

All of them gave a different answer although most of them were practically of the same kind: "The tenants have not cleaned the room for some time." "The owner was a careless person." "The people who used it were dirty and lazy." "The room was not being used."

However, one student was very positive and wrote: "There had been a spider in the room".

THOUGHT

The story tells us that for the same question the teacher received different answers. Most of them were on the negative side, however one was positive.

In like manner, a problem, a burden, an affliction can be viewed in different ways, depending on the positive or negative frame of mind of the persons involved.

There is much pessimism in the world. Let us try some optimism instead.

Above all, let us strive to cultivate the right attitude, and take care not to apply any interpretation by which we may harm or hurt others irresponsibly.

PRAYER

O Lord God, help us to concentrate on the true facts of a situation without being overly critical.

Inspire us to be effective as much as possible in advocating the good points we notice in any difficult situation we may encounter, so that we won't have time to dwell on the bad side.

May we, as far as possible, seek the positive and constructive side of everything.

Help us to have a pleasing attitude at all times, pleasing above all in your sight.

QUOTATION

Two cooks can take precisely the same ingredients and out of them one can make a revolting mess and the other an appetising delight.

(William Barclay)

71

HAPPINESS

ANECDOTE: THE KING AND THE SHIRT

An old story says that there was a king who was dying of melancholy. Many doctors were called and tried every cure but to no avail.

After consulting among themselves, the doctors unanimously suggested to the king that his melancholy could be cured if he managed to procure and wear the shirt of a perfectly happy man.

Hence a search was launched throughout the king's realm to find a perfectly happy man.

At last they found such a man. He happened to be a tramp on the road, tranquil, carefree, utterly happy. They offered to pay him any amount of money he cared to ask for his shirt – only to find out that he was not wearing any shirt at all.

THOUGHT

Are we among those people who think that happiness comes from the material things we succeed to obtain? Let us hope it is not so.

May we be convinced that no place, no person, nothing,

can make us happy. We may live in a hut or in a palace, we may be poor or rich, we may be living with this or that person; it is only we, in union with God's holy will, who can make ourselves happy. It is not in the power of things to bring happiness to anyone.

God alone does not change. In him our soul overflows with happiness.

PRAYER

O Lord God, make us wise to realise that no happiness will last unless it springs from within our own soul.

Make us also understand that if we depend for our happiness on things around us, then we are altogether at their mercy, totally dependent on them. It means that as long as they are with us we are happy, but as soon as they disappear happiness flies off with them.

Convince us that the way to lasting happiness is the right relationship with our inner self united to your holy will.

QUOTATION

The heart is rich when it is content, and it is always content when its desires are fixed on God. Nothing can bring greater happiness than doing God's will for the love of God.

(Miguel F. Cordero)

72

FACING PROBLEMS

ANECDOTE: SOME PAPER AND A PENCIL

In a secondary school the students were having a football match when an accident occurred. One of the boys had a very bad fall and broke his right arm.

When he was waiting for the ambulance to take him to the hospital, he asked for a piece of paper and a pencil.

The teacher asked: "What on earth you need paper and pencil for at this moment?"

The boy's answer was: "Well, instead of killing the time waiting for the ambulance, I thought that I had better start at once learning to write with my left hand as well."

THOUGHT

The opportunity to learn writing with his left hand was no doubt forced on the boy by the problem he had to face unexpectedly.

One of the things in this world which we do well to keep in mind is, that every problem may bring either an opportunity or a disaster. It all depends on how we take it.

The boy decided that his broken hand would not be a disaster and get him down, rather he wisely and courageously decided to take it as a good opportunity to start learning to write with his left hand.

Prayer

O Lord God, we ask you to orient our minds towards positive thinking, especially when facing a problem, so that we may become more conscious of our ability to notice good opportunities, and even to create them.

We know that your expectations of us are not meant to be burdens, but rather invitations to gain and benefit from them that we may lead a better and a more mature life.

When we find ourselves in difficult circumstances may we be brave enough to handle the ones that we can, and to trust you to handle with us the ones that we cannot manage just by ourselves.

Quotation

When fate throws a knife at you, you can catch it by the blade and severely wound yourself, or you can catch it by the handle and use it to carve a new future for yourself.

(J. B. Cabell)

73

SIN'S FOLLY

ANECDOTE: THE LITTLE GIRL WHO WAS LOST

One morning a woman went out shopping taking her six-year-old daughter along with her.

All of a sudden the girl went missing. The frantic mother notified the police who immediately started searching for the child.

After some time, a policeman came across a little girl answering to the description of the lost child. He approached her and very gently asked her: "Little girl, aren't you lost?"

The child looked straight into the face of the policeman and spoke with dignity: "I'm not lost. I just don't know where my mother is."

THOUGHT

Regrettably there are times in our life when like that little girl we too get lost. We get lost when we drift away from God by our sins.

Fortunately for us, God, like that little girl's mother, as soon as we drift away from him, will immediately start searching, so to say, for us.

He will use every possible way and means to make us, his erring children, realise our awful mistake and He will also help us to return to him.

PRAYER

O Lord God, like that little child we have all gone astray, got lost, sometime or other. What is worse, we are all capable of going astray from you again at any moment.

If we had only your justice to deal with we might well despair, but we know, however, that we are dealing with your infinite mercy. Above all we know that you love us with a love we cannot grasp or understand.

For the number of times we were lost by our sins, we ask you to pardon us. We thank you for calling and accepting us back to you. We promise to do our utmost not to allow any sin to separate us from you.

QUOTATION

At times one must wonder how any man who knows of God's generosity and of what that generosity has led him to do for us, could ever think of abandoning that loving God, or get lost in futile earthly folly. Yet that does happen when we sin grievously.

(Kevin O'Sullivan)

74

DECEIVED

ANECDOTE: THE TWO LITTLE BROTHERS

Two little brothers aged six and five, climbed up on a stool and reached for two jars that appeared to them to be a new kind of jam.

They scooped large portions out of the jars and spread it thickly on slices of bread. They were eating to their hearts' content when suddenly their mother came in.

When the mother discovered what the children were doing she became frantic and immediately removed the jars from their hands. She rushed out to a neighbour asking him to drive her and her two sons to the hospital.

She was in time to save their lives because the jars did not contain jam but rat poison.

THOUGHT

What the jars actually contained was completely different from what the children had thought it to be.

Surely in our life too, there were times when what we thought we had heard was not actually what was said. Again, haven't we had the experience that the person or the thing we thought we had seen was actually very different from the reality. And weren't there occasions when we misunderstood others?

Unlike children, we have no excuse for not investigating thoroughly all things before being able to assert their right or wrong condition.

Let us be on our guard not to allow anyone or anything to deceive us, and above all let us be careful that we may not deceive ourselves.

PRAYER

O Lord God, you know that there are many things that appear harmless to us while actually they are poisons. Surely, there are more than physical poisons around us. There are many things that appear harmless to us, but they are actually moral or spiritual pitfalls.

Help us to have our mind in the right place so that we may always be able to discern what is right from what is wrong, what is good from what is bad. Grant us the grace to see clearly what is bodily or spiritually beneficial or harmful to us.

QUOTATION

The devil first deceives you, then he laughs at you and tells everybody about it.

(Maltese Proverb)

75

SELFISHNESS

ANECDOTE: THE FATHER DIDN'T LIKE FISHING

The father did not like to fish at all. So when one day his son asked him to take him fishing he was very much less than enthusiastic.

However, the next day, just before dawn, he and his son woke up and hurried to the seashore.

The son was very excited but his father was not at all. In fact when about an hour had passed without a bite he was so bored that he left his son alone and went to the car where he promptly fell asleep.

Not much later the son, very disappointed, went to the car and asked his father to take him home. He murmured: "I'll never ask you again. Next time I'll come with somebody else."

THOUGHT

Our natural instinct of selfishness impels us to think only of ourselves without any concern for others.

When our ego is in conflict with those of others, we cannot satisfy the one without injuring the other.

Let us strive to expel selfishness from our mind and

try never to miss an opportunity of helping others even at the cost of a big sacrifice.

PRAYER

O Lord God, you know that because of our selfishness we become blind and thus fail to see the needs of others.

Help us to struggle always against the spirit of selfishness that may stifle our impulses to kindliness.

Help us to get rid of the obsession we have of our rights, and let us start thinking of the rights of others.

May we eradicate from ourselves the indifference towards others, that indifference that springs from the vicious depths of selfishness and manifests itself in utter lack of consideration for the needs of others.

May we cultivate in us at least a little consideration for the wellbeing of others.

QUOTATION

The one important thing I have learnt over the years is the difference between taking one's work seriously and taking oneself seriously. The first is imperative – the second is disastrous.

(Dame M. Fonteyn)

76

GRATITUDE

ANECDOTE: A HELPING HAND

Late one night a young man was driving along an isolated road when the motor of the car stopped as it ran out of petrol.

Another driver travelling on the same road came along and asked if he could offer a helping hand.

In fact he did help by offering some petrol from the tank of his own car.

When the first driver insisted to pay, the stranger adamantly refused.

"How am I to show you my appreciation for your kindness?" the first driver asked.

The fellow traveller replied: "If you really want to show your gratitude, any time you are driving, don't fail to stop and offer your help to anyone you may meet stranded on the road."

THOUGHT

Gratitude consists in a warm and friendly feeling towards a benefactor thereby showing appreciation for the gift or favour received. The appreciation may be shown in various ways.

When we show gratitude for receiving a kind deed, we bring happiness not only to the person who has done the favour but also to ourselves.

An ungrateful person cannot be happy, much less make anyone else happy. Let us endow ourselves by the richness of gratitude!

May we have a grateful heart!

PRAYER

O Lord God, giver of every good and perfect gift, put into our hearts gratitude for all that you give us either directly or through the generosity of others.

Help us to be more aware of your goodness that so often comes to us through the people and through the things in life you allow us to enjoy. Deepen our appreciation for your gifts.

Enable us to express our gratitude to you not merely by words, but by giving help to those in difficulties, by our kindness to those in need, and by sympathising with those whose heart is sore and sad.

QUOTATION

There is no lovelier way to thank God for your sight, than by giving a helping hand to someone in the dark.

(Helen Keller)

77

OUR UPS AND DOWNS

ANECDOTE: "WHO CAN SAY?"

A poor farmer lost trace of the only horse he had. When the villagers came to know about it, they sympathized with the farmer and said: "Bad luck!"

The farmer answered: "Bad Luck! Good Luck! Who can say?"

On the next day, the horse returned home with ten other horses. When the villagers heard the good news, they said to the farmer: "Good luck!"

The farmer replied: "Good luck! Bad luck! Who can say?"

Later that day, his only son fractured his leg while training one of the new horses. Again the villagers consoled the farmer by saying: "Bad luck!" He replied: "Bad luck! Good luck! Who can say?"

Few days later, a group of bandits surprised the village and took all the young men away captives, except the farmer's son because of his fractured leg.

THOUGHT

It does happen sometimes, that we think a happy experience is going to occur but its opposite takes place. For instance we expect to be freed completely from worries, and more trouble comes our way.

Again, sometimes we think that we are heading towards what seems to be a disaster for us, and we find that it is a fortune.

The constant flow of positives and negatives is a paradox that most of us have to experience in our lives.

Joy and sorrow like spring and autumn succeed each other without fail.

PRAYER

O Lord God, we know fully well that just as the day with its bright light changes into night with its pitch darkness and back again, so also the times of light and darkness in our lives constantly flow into one another.

May we have the insight and strength to go through the ups and downs of life with a calm and peaceful mind.

Help us to be brave not to allow ourselves to wear out by either of them, knowing that this continuous cycle of change will go on unremittingly in some way or other till the end of our sojourn in this world.

QUOTATION

While we are awaiting some consolation, the cross is already coming up the stairs.

(Maltese Proverb)

78

ACCEPTANCE

ANECDOTE: THE NURSE AND THE LITTLE CHILD

A couple and their little daughter were travelling home after spending a holiday on the mountains. Unfortunately their car was involved in a serious accident that necessitated the amputation of the girl's right leg.

After the operation the child, with tears flowing from her eyes, pleaded with the nurse to pray that God would restore her leg.

The nurse held the little girl in her arms and fervently prayed that God would be with her, and that he would help her to live her life as best she could, irrespective of the way it turned out to be.

THOUGHT

With every probability, we all wish that God would spare us suffering, little do we realise that often it is we ourselves or may be others who bring suffering upon us. God just has to permit it.

No doubt we can use every legitimate means to remove our pain and suffering but if we fail, may it not lead us to self pity or despair, but to a selfless kind of love and compassion for others in their suffering.

What we see as tragedies may be only blessings in disguise, and may also be the very opportunities through which God chooses to shower upon us and through us upon others his love and grace.

PRAYER

O Lord God, we pray that we may never have to go through a tragedy similar to the one that the little girl had to go through. May we never have to suffer at all. But if ever we will have to suffer, as most probably we will have to, may we then be able to turn to you and ask you to perform the miracle to peacefully accept those things that we will not be able to change.

Help us to be able to find new joy in our night of sorrow, and also unexpected grace in our time of need.

We ask you that whenever we find ourselves shrouded in the darkness of adversity, do not allow us to despair, rather by your grace show us that we can still be calm and peaceful.

QUOTATION

It is our Maker who 'gives songs in the night'. If we wait on him for the music, we'll find there is never a song so sweet as his 'midnight melodies'.

(Henry G. Bosch)

79

PRIDE

ANECDOTE: THE FROG AND THE GEESE

A frog was planning how to get away from the cold winter climate. "I've got a splendid brain! I know what I'll do," he said to himself. Then he approached two geese that soon would start on their migrating journey to a warmer country. "I would like to migrate with you," he told them. In amazement the geese responded: "But you can't fly!"

"I surely know! But I have a plan," the frog retorted. "You pick up a strong reed, each holding one end, and I'll hold on to it with my mouth."

The geese agreed and in due time the three of them started on their journey. Soon they were passing over a small town and someone cried out: "Look, look! Who could have conceived such a clever idea?"

Hearing this, the frog got so puffed up with a sense of importance that he opened his mouth, and before he could boast: "I planned it," he lost his hold on the reed and fell to his death.

THOUGHT

As wisdom is the most perfect of man's virtues, so pride is the worst of his vices. If we reflect for a moment we see that to be proud is to be very foolish.

The foolishness of pride can be seen very clearly in others when we notice them fishing for compliments after getting some achievements, and trying hard to draw the attention of everyone upon themselves because of their own imagined importance.

Let us learn that what we detest in others we must avoid from ourselves.

PRAYER

O Lord God, we understand that it is not pride at all to be conscious of our talents, provided that we use them for your greater glory and for the good of others and of ourselves.

It becomes pride if we arrogate to ourselves these powers and pretend that they are all our doing, and thus seek honour and glory exclusively for ourselves.

Provide us with the humility, which will keep us from pride and from conceit. May we be gracious and gentle, so that we will be both easy to live with and a joy to meet. Forgive us our sins we have committed through pride.

QUOTATION

Pride goes before destruction, and haughtiness before a fall.

(Proverbs 16:18)

80

TRUST

A husband bought a gift to give it to his wife as a present on her birthday.

On his return home he found his little daughter, whose legs were paralysed, sitting in her wheelchair. As she noticed her father going upstairs with the parcel in his hands to give it to his wife who was doing some house work, she immediately asked him: "Dad, may I carry the parcel to mum myself?"

"How can you possibly carry it when you can't even carry yourself?" her father told her kindly.

"It's so simple, papa! Give me the parcel to hold in my hands and then you may please carry me near mum," the girl answered with a broad smile on her face.

That is exactly what her father did.

THOUGHT

Because of her trust in her father's love for her, the girl fulfilled her heart's desire in spite of her serious handicap.

God never promised that our life would be without conflicts, but He did promise to be with us through them.

He has even promised to help us that we would be victorious over them if only we approach him and then rely on his love for us. We just have to believe in this challenge.

The trouble with us, is that we are afraid to trust. Yet trust in God is the surest chance we have to experience peace and comfort in times of trial.

PRAYER

O Lord God, in the midst of our difficulties, frailties and failures may we have confidence in your goodness towards us.

We are aware that to have a complete trust in you is probably the most difficult thing asked of us. For this reason we beg you to give us that very important gift of an unwavering trust and confidence in you.

As we stand here today we bring you all our confidence of which we are capable. We know that this is the gift that you most appreciate from us.

May our trust in you become stronger. Above all, may it remain strong in the midst of the dark and weak moments of our life.

QUOTATION

Trust is the greatest joy in our relationship with God. Whoever trusts in God has already covered the hardest part of the journey... God, you are my God, I can count on you.

(Carlo Carretto)

81

UNDERSTANDING

ANECDOTE: THE FARMER AND THE BAKER

A baker decided to buy the butter used in his trade from a local farmer. After some time, he noticed that the weight of butter in the packages was reduced and yet he was still paying the same price as before.

Getting annoyed at this deception, the baker took the farmer to court accusing him of cheating and fraud.

In court the judge asked the farmer: "What measuring weights do you make use of?" The farmer answered: "I don't have any."

Then the judge wanted to know: "In that case, how do you manage to weigh the butter that you sell?"

"Very easy," the farmer was quick to answer, "When the baker began buying the butter from me, I thought that I'd better buy my bread from him. And from that time I used to weigh my butter according to the weight of his bread. If the weight of my butter is wrong, then he has only to blame himself."

THOUGHT

We often have misconceptions about why people are the way they are, or why they act as they act, or why they talk the way they talk. This is especially true when we are hurt or irritated by the behaviour of others. Little do we care to realise that we ourselves may be the cause of their attitude being what it is.

We should always try to understand others rather than judging them because we just cannot judge; our judgement may easily be the wrong one.

PRAYER

O Lord God, grant us an understanding mind and a suppleness of heart that we might associate more lovingly with others.

Give us the gift of understanding, and help us to avoid jumping into the wrong conclusions by judging others.

If we feel that there is a scope for change in others, help us to use the proper approach with much love, respect and consideration.

By our understanding may we be the source of much love, peace and joy.

QUOTATION

Be not disturbed at being misunderstood; be disturbed rather at not being understanding.

(Chinese Proverb)

82

BURDENS

There is a story about a young girl who was climbing up a hill carrying an invalid child on her shoulders.

A man who happened to be passing by remarked to her: "Lass, that's a pretty heavy burden for you to carry!"

The girl looked at him with a radiant face and replied: "Sir, it's not really a burden. It's my young brother."

THOUGHT

No one of us goes through this life without having any burden. Burdens can be anything from physical and mental handicaps to worries, anxieties, frustrations, loneliness, and other undesirable things like these.

The weight of a burden depends on the way we look at it. A burden may not seem to be heavy when it is precious to us, though undoubtedly it will still be hard to bear, causing us to suffer pain, perplexity and fear.

May we never rebel against the burden that we cannot get rid of, because if we do, then we may make it unbearable, and we may even allow despair to take hold of us and thus destroy completely the peace within us and around us.

Prayer

O Lord God, when we feel that our burden is heavy, help us to bravely shoulder our load and to determinedly struggle on our way towards you.

We realise that certain difficulties and sufferings cannot be changed or be healed no matter what we do about them. In spite of all our efforts they may remain bad and perhaps they may even worsen. In such terrible moments may we have the grace and courage to remain united with you trusting in your comfort and succour, hence we will not lose our peace and tranquillity.

In our seemingly very dark moments, do not let us be tempted to doubt that light would ever return to our life. Rather teach us to have recourse to you and to believe in your love, your presence, and your power.

Quotation

The difficulties of life are intended to make us better, not bitter.

(George Gritter)

83

GOD'S LOVE

ANECDOTE: THE WEATHERCOCK

A farmer placed a weathercock inscribed with the sentence "God is love" on top of his barn.

One day a traveller, noticing the weathercock, stopped to look, and with a smirk on his face asked the farmer standing at the door of the farm: "Do you think that God's love can change so lightly like the vane you've got up there?"

Smilingly the farmer shook his head and replied: "No, my friend! That is meant to show that whichever way the wind blows, 'God is love'."

THOUGHT

Can a woman forget her own baby and not love the child she bore? Yet even if a mother should forget her child, God will never forget us.

God has our names not just written but engraved on the palms of his hands. He knows each one of us by our name. He knows us inside out.

During those moments in which everything seems to go wrong, or in those moments full of misunderstandings, we can rely on his love. He surely demonstrates his love for us, regardless of the circumstances in which we may find ourselves.

The trouble rests with us, in the sense that either we may not fully believe what this kind of love can really be, or that we may forget about it.

Prayer

O Lord God, your love for us seems to be too good to be true. May we ask you to deepen our consciousness of this fact, that is of your immense love for each and every one of us, and help us to fully trust in it.

Your promise of your love for us is continuously with us; it has just to be accepted by us.

We know that we will never be able to plumb the depths of your love – not even in eternity. Yet we dare to pray that our minds may realise how much we stand to gain through your love for us, and also that our hearts may be wide open to receive it willingly and gratefully.

Quotation

I believe that God loves each one of us without condition, no matter what we ever do or say or think or feel. We are free to accept that love, respond to that love, or reject that love and try to go it alone.

(Nina Herrmann)

84

CONTENTMENT

ANECDOTE: THE ROBIN AND THE WORMS

Early one winter, on a dreary and rainy morning, the headmaster of a secondary school looked out of his office window and noticed a robin perching on a branch of an apple tree.

As the headmaster was admiring the beautiful bird, all of a sudden he saw it flying down on the grass below.

He watched it snatching three worms one after the other from the grass, swallowing them very swiftly, and then flying up to the previous place on the branch.

There, the robin seemed to be very contented and satisfied, as he began to sing. His song was surely his rendition of "Praise the Lord".

THOUGHT

The robin seemed to be delighted with what Providence had provided for him. He did not complain about the colour or size or taste of the worms. He was simply contented and satisfied. What a lesson for many of us!

How many people there are who are never satisfied with anything they have! They constantly grasp, covet, and seek to obtain what does not pertain to them. Such people think, as the saying goes, that the grass is always greener on the other side of the fence.

It seems that they do not realise the folly of their discontentment. How absolutely miserable and unhappy they make themselves unnecessarily!

PRAYER

O Lord God, we ask you to endow us with the upright attitude to be grateful and appreciative for the benefits we receive, thereby we cherish how green the grass is on our side of the fence.

Let us never fall in that category of people who are never contented with their lot, even when they have a lot more than what they need. Spare us from being affected by such an inordinate conduct!

Help us to meditate seriously on the question: "What good are the gifts of life if we do not appreciate and enjoy their goodness?"

QUOTATION

I do not possess anything that I do not want, and I do not want anything that I do not possess.

(Daniel Defoe)

85

HYPOCRISY

ANECDOTE: THE YOUNG SALESGIRL

On the birthday of his wife, the husband walked into a gift shop to buy a present for her.

The young salesgirl greeted him with a cheery: "Good day!" She talked to him very pleasantly, took him round the shop, helped him to choose a suitable present and neatly wrapped his purchase.

Before leaving the shop he casually asked the salesgirl: "You must really be very happy doing this kind of work!"

To which, to his great surprise, she replied: "Actually, I hate it. Right now I'm counting the minutes till my time to stay here is up, so that I can join my friends on the beach."

THOUGHT

We may say: "How strange for the girl to be able to behave so sweetly when she was so bitter inside her! What a good actress she was! She succeeded in giving the impression that she enjoyed her work while in reality she hated it."

Is it actually strange? Let us have a look at ourselves

*and see if in the past we too somehow or other have
acted in like manner, or worse still if we are right now
being great pretenders.*

*With every probability, if we are truly sincere with
ourselves, we realise that often we pretend to be good
and honest and holy, but in our hearts there is wickedness,
bitterness, dishonesty and pride.*

PRAYER

O Lord God, you know fully well that there are times in
our life, not to say most of the time, when we behave like
that salesgirl, when we are actors, pretenders, two-faced,
yes hypocrites, that is to say putting on an external show
while inwardly our thoughts and feelings are very
different.

We know that by our external show we may bluff,
cheat or deceive others, but not you. In your sight our
life is like an open page of a book.

You know us infinitely better than we know ourselves.
You see our mind and our heart. You know our thoughts,
our desires and our feelings.

QUOTATION

**For neither man nor angel can discern
Hypocrisy, the only evil that walks
Invisible, except to God alone.**

(John Milton)

86

GOD'S PRESENCE

ANECDOTE: HE WENT TO STEAL POTATOES

The neighbour's field was covered with a very rich crop of potatoes. It proved to be a great temptation for a man living close by. In fact one day he took his small son with him and went to the field to steal some potatoes.

Cautiously the father looked this way and then that way before climbing up the fence.

The son having noticed what his father had done remarked: "Daddy, you forgot something."

"What's it, son?" the father asked very anxiously.

"You didn't look up!" the child replied innocently.

THOUGHT

The fact that before climbing up the fence the father looked around to make sure that he was not being detected, shows he was conscious that he was going to do something wrong.

Sometimes, we may have a strong temptation to snatch some trifle that is lying about, especially if we think that there is no chance of anybody watching us. Though it may be true that there will be little chance of us being detected by anybody, yet it is absolutely true that we will not escape the scrutiny of God, who undoubtedly sees not only our actions but also our feelings, thoughts and desires.

When we have shut the doors and made a darkness within, let us never say that we are alone, for we are not alone, but God is within.

PRAYER

O Lord God, truly you are a hidden God. Though we can very clearly see and admire the wonders of your handicraft, still we cannot see you.

But we are not hidden from you. You see us. In you we live and move and have our being.

Unfortunately when we give in to the temptation of doing what is evil, we seem to forget that the evil is being blatantly done in your presence.

Help us to realise that we should never give in to evil, irrespective of not being seen by anybody. Let us remember that after all, you surely see us.

QUOTATION

The light of God surrounds me, the love of God enfolds me, the power of God protects me, the presence of God watches over me, wherever I am, God is.

(*Words of Encouragement* – D. P. Cronin)

87

THOUGHTFULNESS

ANECDOTE: TWO YOUNG GIRLFRIENDS

Two young girls on very friendly terms decided to go abroad to spend a holiday together. The trouble with them was that one of them hated the cold weather while the other did not like the warm weather.

Before entering the hotel room they agreed to leave its window as they would find it, open if it was open and closed if it was closed. They found the window closed, and both of them went to sleep leaving the window closed.

During the night the girl who loved the warm weather awoke and feeling pity for her friend, got out of her bed and opened the window for some cool breeze to come in for the benefit of her friend.

In the morning when both of them got up they found that the window had no pane glasses at all.

THOUGHT

Both girls were so concerned for each other that they had not even noticed that the window in the room had no glass fixed on it.

The action of the girl breaking their own rule for the sake of the other speaks loudly of their thoughtfulness and sensitivity.

Thoughtfulness is when we think of and care for others more than we think of and care for ourselves; it is when we willingly and gladly forego comfort, pleasure, gain, and so on, for the sake of another.

PRAYER

O Lord God, if we really believe that your love for us is as personal as it actually is, we would surely have you as a friend above all others. How we long to grow in this awareness, though we are conscious that we have a long way to cover.

And once this awareness in us is complete we shall naturally be very mindful of you and very thoughtful of others.

We ask your pardon for the number of times we thought only of ourselves and failed to be considerate towards anybody else. Show us where we need improvement that we may care for others at least as much as we care for ourselves.

QUOTATION

When you have learned even a little thoughtfulness for others, you will have taken a great step forward in cultivating the gift of amiability.

(R. de Saint-Laurent)

88

EXCUSES

ANECDOTE: THE FISHERMAN AND THE TWO FISHES

A man was on the seashore fishing with his rod when presently he caught a big fish. But as he removed it from the hook it slipped from his hand to disappear again into the sea.

Soon afterwards, he got another fish, but it was rather a small one. This time he unhooked it very cautiously, and very carefully put it in his container.

At that moment a man approached the fisherman and asked him: "Why did you throw back into the sea the big fish and then you kept the small one?"

"Because my frying pan is small and it would not hold that big fish," the fisherman was quick to answer.

THOUGHT

The fisherman of the story is a clear example of how difficult it is for us to admit our mistake or to acknowledge that we have committed a blunder or to accept a failure.

Excuses, often silly ones, sometimes even to the point of ridiculing ourselves, come so easily to us. The worst part of it is, that in doing so, we seem not to realize what fools we make of ourselves.

Do we find it very difficult to say "Sorry", "Excuse me", "Pardon me" even when we are absolutely sure that we are at fault?

We seem to forget that if we admit our failures, then God can work wonders through them too, if only we allow him to do so.

PRAYER

O Lord God, you know how prone we are to justify our action however wrong it may be. We are ever ready to excuse ourselves, sometimes even to the extent of trying to get scot-free by shamelessly putting the blame on some innocent person.

Probably, in the past we might have even tried to excuse ourselves with you when we fully knew that no excuse could stand before you.

We seize this opportunity not only to ask you to pardon us for the times we tried to excuse unduly our wrong doing, but also to promise you to try not to do anything wrong in the future. Thereby we will not need any excuses.

QUOTATION

He who excuses himself accuses himself.

(Gabriel Meurier)

89

ADVICE

ANECDOTE: THE STUDENT AND THE PROFESSOR

A student who was anxious to secure a high position in society later on in life was having difficulty with his studies. He was studying hard and doing his best, but he could retain neither what he had read in class nor what he had tried to memorize at home. Thus he approached one of the professors of the college and confided to him. Among other things he told him: "I intend hiring a tutor to help me in my studies."

"No," the professor instructed him, "you don't need a teacher, you need a pupil, someone to whom you will pass on what you study, thereby you will be enhancing your learning."

THOUGHT

The young student acted very wisely when he sought advice from a competent person.

It is quite obvious that when we come face to face with a very serious problem we may not be able to handle it by ourselves. In those moments when difficulties and uncertainties crop up in our life, we would do very

*well to ask a capable and reliable person to walk through
the journey of life along with us.*

*Let us remember that a wise person will not necessarily
be able to solve our problem, but he or she can point out
to us what our options are towards an acceptable solution.*

PRAYER

O Lord God, we are aware that sometimes you choose
wise and conscientious persons to speak to us through
them. For this we thank you with all our heart.

Help us to discard the illusion we may be having that
we do not need any advisers, and grant us the humility
we need to be able to accept with gratitude a wise advice
when it is offered to us.

Make us understand that when we seek advice, we
increase our possibilities of successfully choosing the
right answer. After all someone else often detects what
we cannot.

QUOTATION

**Advice is seldom welcome; and those who want it the
most always like it the least.**

(Chesterfield)

90

REPAYING IN KIND

One early morning, on a radio station, before the newscaster, who was a part-time employee, began to read out the news he wished a good day to the three other persons present in the newsroom whom he mentioned by name and to all the radio listeners.

Then he said: "As I finish reading the news I've to dash to my place of work."

The voice of one of the three was heard saying: "We shall not miss you at all."

To which the newsreader repaid him in kind: "Nor will I."

THOUGHT

The slightly unkind remark passed by one of the three persons was no doubt, out of place. It had hurt somewhat the feelings of the newscaster.

On the other hand it would have been better if the newscaster did not repay the injury. It would have been better still if he did not even show that he had got offended. After all, he gained nothing by retaliating.

The person who thinks he must return every unkind word addressed to him, or repay any hurtful deed that is directed towards him, will have a profitless job. Probably, in the end he will be the one who will suffer most.

PRAYER

O Lord God, help us to be gracious in our attitude towards others even when theirs towards us is not as it should be.

We know that the spirit of the world enjoins us to get even with those who mistreat us. We know also that you tell us to love our enemies, to bless those who curse us, and to do good to those who hate us.

Help us to have the strength and the courage to be always kind, patient, considerate, and loving in our words and actions towards everyone including those who are not so nice towards us.

In whatever circumstances, and with whomever we may find ourselves to be, let us always try to be successful healers and peacemakers.

QUOTATION

He who throws mud at another not only gets his hands dirty but he also loses his own soil.

(English Saying)

91

THANKFULNESS

ANECDOTE: TWO COLLEGE STUDENTS

During the Annual College Sports Day two college student-classmates took part in a slow cycle-race. One of them lost his balance and while he was falling he hit another participant who happened to be the other classmate, and together went toppling down to the ground.

Both of them fractured a leg, one his right leg, the other his left one. Since during the first few days after the incident they could not attend the college, every day they phoned separately from their respective homes to the Prefect of their class asking him for the notes and homework assignments.

When later on they started attending the college, one of them took a small gift and presented it to the Prefect in appreciation of the help he had given him. The other did not even bother to say 'Thank you'.

THOUGHT

Let us ask ourselves: "Of the two students whom would we imitate if we had to pass through similar circumstances as they had gone through?"

Let us hope that our answer is definitely and emphatically: "We would follow the very fine attitude of the one who was thankful".

May we be always sensitive to the favours bestowed upon us, leading us to express appreciation even for the smallest services received from God, our family, our friends and even from the society or the state.

PRAYER

O Lord God, help us to cultivate in us the sense of being thankful.

May we be conscious to the necessity of being indebted to those who show us kindness and sympathy, thereby awaking in us a deep sense of thankfulness towards all our benefactors and well-wishers and also impelling us to be thoughtful of and to do good to others.

Eradicate completely from our hearts all selfish, inconsiderate and insensitive feelings towards others, and in their place plant the virtues of thoughtfulness, thankfulness and benevolence.

QUOTATION

God has two dwellings – one in heaven and the other in a thankful heart.

(Isaak Walton)

92

GOD'S POWER

ANECDOTE: WAS THE TIGER STILL WILD?

A young man captured a tiger cub, brought it home, and raised it in a big cage. When the tiger became fully grown, its owner used to brag with friends and neighbours what a ferocious and powerful animal it was.

"Your tiger can't be wild anymore," scoffed a friend. "He's as tame as an old house cat."

An old man overheard them and said: "To know whether this tiger is ferocious or not, you need only open its cage."

The young man accepted this suggestion, placed his hand on the latch, and challenged his friend: "Stay here and try out my tiger."

The friend did not stand there but ran for his life.

THOUGHT

A tiger uses its strength to destroy, to hurt, to kill, to devour, but God uses his power very differently. Every touch of God's power is a grace.

Sometimes it brings consolation and peace; sometimes it removes the guilt of sin, brings forgiveness, and breaks

*the grips of bad and evil habits; at other times it touches
us with darkness so that we might love God for himself
rather than for his favours.*

*When God touches us by his power, let us admit our
weakness, and stay true to God thereby giving him a
chance to reveal his graces to us.*

PRAYER

O Lord God, enable us to understand the meaning of
your divine power in our lives, and to realise that every
time you exercise this power upon us, is a sure sign of
your love.

We know that you tailor each touch of your power
upon us according to our individual and particular needs.

Though we may not understand what every exercise
of your power upon us means, help us to discern the love
and healing that each one of them contains.

QUOTATION

**I can assure you that nothing became more real to me
in prison than the certainty that I was not alone. Day
after day when I should have been planning suicide, I
would feel the sustaining power of God. ... What was
true of me was true of the others.**

(F. Olin. Stockwell)

93

GOD'S VOICE

ANECDOTE: CHILD, MOTHER AND COOKIES

A 5-year-old child walked into the kitchen, finding his mother baking cookies. He stood watching her. After a while he hopefully asked: "Mummy, may I please have one?"

"Not before supper, my son" his mother replied.

The child sulked and ran tearfully to his room. Very soon he returned with a message: "God just told me it's okay to have a cookie now."

"But God didn't tell me that!" his mother retorted.

To which the child was quick to reply: "You must have not been listening."

THOUGHT

The child was wrong in asking to have cookies before supper. Still he said that God had spoken to him and agreed with him. It was his imagination or probably he had made up things. God does not inspire us to wrongdoing.

The mother, who was right in not giving cookies to her son before having his supper, declared that she had not heard God. Her son insisted that God had spoken to her too, but she had not heard.

How will we come to hear the voice of God and recognise it as such?

Listening and recognising God's voice come when we decide to spend some quiet time with him in prayer. After laying bare before him our thoughts and desires then we can hear clearly his response.

PRAYER

O Lord God, we regrettably acknowledge that most of us, through much of our life, have not heard your voice calling us and talking to us.

In this regard, we are very sure about two things, that you do speak to us, and that we need to hear it.

We assure you that we long to hear you speaking to us, hence we humbly ask you to help us to discern your voice.

We also know fully well that by listening to your voice we will be the gainers; our profit will be enormous for body and soul. So help us, Lord, to hear your voice and recognise it whenever you speak to us!

QUOTATION

For he is the Lord our God; and we are the people of his pasture, and the sheep of his hand. Today if you will hear his voice, harden not your hearts.

(Psalm 95: 7-8)

94

COMPASSION

ANECDOTE: THE GLOVES AND THE MUFFLER

An old lady climbed onto a train and took the nearest seat available. She was poorly dressed and she had barely anything to protect her from the bitter winter wind. Her tired, cracked, bony hands were holding an old, tattered, worn out shawl tightly around her shoulders.

At the next stop, a young man and his girlfriend strode onto the train. They were well dressed and well protected against the cold weather.

Two stops later, as the train slowed, the couple passed very close to the old lady, and got down from the train.

On the lap of the old lady lay the young man's leather gloves and the girl's woollen muffler.

THOUGHT

To what extent do we share with others in need from the abundance of our own possessions and thereby putting compassion in action?

That young couple saw the poor, shivering old lady, and responded with compassion. While so many others had also seen her and still it never occurred to them to help her in any way.

It is true that we cannot help everyone, but do we actually help those whom we can help?

Undoubtedly, we would like others to show compassion to us if we were in need. Then it is only right that we try to develop greater compassion to others.

PRAYER

O Lord God, help us to be sensitive to the needs of others by reaching out and giving even a little of what we have.

Let us keep in mind that we show our love for you by what we do with what we have. Yes, we demonstrate it when performing acts of compassion to your people, those who are in need, the poor, the miserable, the hungry, the destitute.

Make us realise that compassion is not just feeling sorry for people; it is a heartache so intense that it inspires us and moves us into action.

QUOTATION

The compassion that you see in the kind-hearted is God's own compassion: he has given it to them to protect the helpless.

(Sri Ramakrishna)

95

BELIEF IN GOD

ANECDOTE: SHE AND HER RELIGION

Someone approached a woman belonging to a particular religion of which she had been a staunch member for many years, and asked her: "Tell me, just what do you believe?"

She replied coolly: "I believe what my religion believes."

"But what does your religion believe?" was the next question put to her.

She quickly answered: "My religion believes what I believe."

The inquirer asked her: "Since you believe what your religion believes, and your religion believes what you believe, what do you and your religion believe?"

She answered: "Most certainly, we both believe the same thing."

THOUGHT

Do we ever question the raison d'etre of what we are accustomed to do? Perhaps we are satisfied by the way of life we are living, whether it is about religion or politics or education or even about the food we eat.

With every probability our belief in God was infused in us through the society in which we live, especially the parents of our family. But that should not be the raison d'etre of our belief.

The existence of God is not simply a guess or an act of faith in what someone has infused in us. We should be convinced of it and that conviction must come from our heart, and we do not need special cleverness or education to have it.

PRAYER

O Lord God, we confess that our belief in you may not be great, but we boldly and proudly profess that we believe in a great God.

We pray for such a strong belief in you that will enliven our lives in a way that it will also bring hope and joy to the lives of others.

We ask not only for an increase in our belief in you but more so to trust enthusiastically in your magnificent providence, love and mercy.

May we become more aware of your love and presence radiating in our souls. May others too, on their own initiative come to believe ardently in you.

QUOTATION

Lord, I believe; help my unbelief. For I believe in your deep love and mercy, in your forgiving understanding of the human heart.

(Randle Manwaring)

96

THE UNEXPECTED

ANECDOTE: WHILE CHEWING NUTS

Six young boys in their teens were sitting at a round table munching nuts, like peanuts, hazelnuts and cashew nuts, and enjoying a soft drink. Suddenly the teeth of one of the boys crunched on something other than a nut, and like lightning, a stab of pain shot through his mouth.

Spitting immediately the nuts out of his mouth, he found among them a small pebble and a piece of a broken tooth.

THOUGHT

We do not associate a broken tooth with chewing nuts. If it happens, as in the case of the teenager, it surely happens very rarely. Undoubtedly, the boy and his friends did not expect it to happen at all.

Incidents like this one, bigger ones perhaps, and even tragic ones, sometimes catch us off guard.

Weren't there any incidents in our lives – pleasant or unpleasant ones – that came upon us like a bolt from the blue? Whatever it was, let us keep in mind that no matter what we do, the twists and turns of life's surprises are going to touch us somehow or other, sometime or another.

PRAYER

O Lord God, help us to realise that the unexpected seems to be an integral part of our lives and therefore we should be prepared for surprises.

Some of the surprises may have a touch of comedy about them, but others may prove to be tragic. In the latter cases help us not to succumb under their weight, but by your grace may we be able to face them bravely and with courage so that we will manage to take such difficulties at our stride.

We understand fully well that what happens unexpectedly to us, has been foreseen by you, and actually happens under your all-seeing vision, not necessarily that you will it but that you may just permit it.

No doubt, your close support will not be lacking.

QUOTATION

As to moral courage, I have very rarely met with the two o'clock in the morning kind. I mean unprepared courage, that which is necessary on an unexpected occasion, and which, in spite of the most unforeseen events, leaves full freedom of judgement and decision.

(Napoleon Bonaparte)

97

SLEEP

ANECDOTE: THE TWO FISHERMEN

Two men had been out at deep-sea fishing.

While heading back towards the land, the more experienced seaman very tired, began to feel sleepy and turned the helm over to his companion.

Some time later the man at his task also fell asleep.

All of a sudden the two fishermen got up with a big fright as the fishing boat ran aground and got stuck, to their good luck, on a sandy beach.

THOUGHT

Sleep is a state of the body and mind such as that, which normally recurs for a number of hours during the night, then the nervous system is inactive, the eyes closed, the muscles and the nerves are relaxed, and consciousness is almost entirely suspended.

Though sleep can be of enormous benefit for us, as it is actually intended to be by our Creator, still it may also be of a great detriment to us. This occurs when we misuse it by idling away our time in unnecessary long sleep, thereby neglecting our work, duties, commitments and other relevant good deeds.

May all of us be wise enough to make the best use of sleep for both body and soul.

We sleep in peace knowing that God is awake; He never sleeps nor slumbers.

Prayer

O Lord God, in your infinite wisdom you have divided the 24-hour day into two parts, one with enough hours of light so that we could work and do whatever is essential for our living, and the other part with enough hours of darkness so that we could have enough sleep to recuperate our strength and to be fit enough for the following day's labour.

May we never be workaholic to the extent of taxing our physical system by depriving it of its deserved and needed restful sleep.

We ask you to help us that every time we lay our head on the pillow to sleep for the hours of the night we do so with a clean conscience.

Quotation

Sleep is the only medicine that gives ease.

(Sophocles)

98

TREASURE

ANECDOTE: THE RARE FLOWER

A group of botanists was exploring a remote part of the country searching for wild flowers to enumerate them to their list.

At one moment, one of the botanists noticed a flower, which was metres down on the side of the cliff. It was very beautiful and seemed to be very rare. To get it, someone had to be lowered down the cliff by means of a rope.

It struck one of the botanists to approach a young boy who happened to be in a field close by and told him that he would pay him very well if he agreed to be lowered to retrieve the flower for him.

"Give me one minute," the boy responded. A little while later he returned together with a middle aged man and said: "I'm ready to go down the cliff and get the flower for you if this man holds the rope. He is my father."

THOUGHT

The meaning of a treasure in this context refers to a person or anything else greatly valued. For instance finding a true friend is finding a treasure. So also, discovering a new flower was for the scientists finding a treasure, and that is why they decided to do whatever they could possibly do to retrieve it.

Usually we are prepared to do any sacrifice either to obtain or not to lose what is very precious to us.

Prayer

O Lord God, help us not to treasure any person or thing that eventually will render us poor in your sight, but help us to treasure any person or thing that ultimately will enrich us in your estimation.

Help us to take a serious look at all the treasures we think we have. Help us to be bold and brave enough to discard the fake ones and to preserve and endear the real ones.

Make us fully conscious that you are the greatest treasure we can ultimately have. Intensify our ability to love and enjoy you to the utmost.

May we never lose, not even for the shortest moment, this greatest treasure of all, that of having faith in and loving you.

Quotation

For where your treasure is, there will your heart be also.

(Matthew 6: 21)

99

GOOD DEED

ANECDOTE: THE GIRL ON THE ROAD

One evening a university student, whose boyfriend was abroad on work, took the car and went for a drive. On the way she met another girl showing the thumb sign, asking for a lift. She stopped and let the girl climb in.

While talking, the girl revealed that she had just broken up with her boyfriend of three years, was feeling inconsolable and consequently she had lost her desire to live.

The university girl suggested a supper together at a nearby restaurant. They became very friendly, joked, laughed, took each other's telephone number and promised to meet again the following evening.

On returning home the university girl heard the telephone ringing. She took it up and to her great surprise heard the voice of the girl whom she had just reached home. "...Under the passenger's seat of your car I've left behind me a plastic bag full of sleeping tablets. I intended to swallow them to commit suicide. You've saved my life..."

THOUGHT

Who knows what would have happened to the girl on the road if the university girl had not stopped the car and given her a lift?

The little good deed she performed led to the two girls to become very friendly, eat, joke, laugh together – and that saved a very precious life.

We should never miss or neglect performing a good deed whenever the occasion arises.

PRAYER

O Lord God, let your light of love, caring, and joy that radiates within us, shine out to others.

May we be your instruments – the salt and the light – to spread peace and happiness to people around us.

We know that people long to be accepted and understood, to know that there is someone who cares about them and is prepared to go along with them through at least a part of their rough life journey. Make us realise that a good deed may do all this and much more.

QUOTATION

How far that little candle throws his beams! So shines a good deed in a naughty world.

(Shakespeare)

100

LOVE

ANECDOTE: A FATHER AND HIS CHILDREN

Two brothers and their younger sister were playing together when suddenly the boys started fighting with each other. Immediately the girl shouted: "If you fight, daddy won't love you!"

On hearing these words, their father, who was doing some work in the adjacent room, left whatever he was doing and came to see what was happening.

The misunderstanding between the two boys was already straightened out. Still their father took the opportunity to reproach them with these words: "I shall always love you. When you do what is right, I love you with a glad heart, and when you do what is wrong, I still love you, but with a sorrowful heart."

THOUGHT

Love like a prism has many facets, such as the love of the parents between themselves, the love of the parents for their children and vice versa, the brotherly and sisterly love, the love of friends for one another, the love of a teacher for the students and vice versa, the sublime love of man for his enemies, and above all our love for God.

Whatever its facet, love is very patient and kind, never jealous or envious, never boastful or proud, never haughty or selfish or rude. It does not demand its own way. It is not irritable or touchy. It does not hold grudges and will hardly even notice when others do it wrong. It is never glad about injustice, but rejoices whenever truth wins out. (1 Cor.13)

PRAYER

O Lord God, keep reminding us that if we are not loving and kind to one another, it shows that we do not love you either.

Increase our faith in the presence of your love that radiates within us and is all around us at every moment.

We know that your love for us would stop at nothing, it is infinite.

May our hearts remain always open to receive your love and to allow it to grow and intensify, so that from them it spreads out to other hearts as well, drawing all the hearts closer together and closer and closer to you.

QUOTATION

Love cures people – both the ones who give it and the ones who receive it.

(Dr. Karl Menninger)

101

PEACE

ANECDOTE: GIVING US HIS GIFT

A little time before leaving this world, just before his passion, death and resurrection, the Lord Jesus Christ had his Last Supper with his apostles.

Surrounded as he was by his intimate friends, among other things he told them: "I am leaving you with a gift – peace of mind and heart! And the peace I give isn't fragile like the peace the world gives. So don't be troubled or afraid." (Jn 14:27)

THOUGHT

Jesus spoke of his gift to the apostles, and surely to all of us, and his gift was peace.

It is quite obvious that by peace he did not mean the absence of war, conflict, division, trouble, and the like. He made it very clear that he meant serenity of mind and heart that nobody and nothing can take away. No sorrow, no danger, no suffering can make it less.

The peace that Jesus gives us does not depend on outward circumstances whatsoever. Circumstances will change, but God will never change. Hence we are convinced that He will always be faithful, and consequently we shall always be at peace.

The peace given to us by Jesus implies God's blessing and friendship.

PRAYER

O Lord God, enable us to live our life so pleasing to you that Jesus may find us worthy to offer us his peace.

We are confident that such peace brings along with it joy, happiness and tranquillity even in moments of sorrow and suffering which we have to experience again and again as we walk through this valley of tears.

May we understand that the peace that Jesus gives us will be given to us because of our right relationship with you; when you come first in our life.

May we conduct ourselves in such a way as to merit this peace, and to be so fortunate as to enjoy it within us.

QUOTATION

Peace of heart – without it no good can make us happy; with it, every trial, even the approach of death, can be borne.

(Frederic Ozanam)

INDEX
[Subjects in alphabetical order]

Other books by the author

Prayers and Thoughts for Students
A Woman's Joys and Other Stories